||||| ||| || |||||| |||| ||||
D0858840

Simply Following

In all my journeying God went before

Betty Ellen Cox

Let's keep on simply following

Betty Ellen Cox

Saltbox Press
Spring Arbor, Michigan

Distributed by:
Free Methodist World Mission People
P. O. Box 535002
Indianapolis, IN 46253-5002

1   3   5   7   9   10   8   6   4   2

Published by Saltbox Press
167 Burr Oak Drive, Spring Arbor, MI 49283
Printed in the United States of America
Autobiography, Missiology, Sanctified Living
ISBN: 1-878559-05-2
Price: $15.00 USA
        $22.50 Canada

Simply Following

In all my journeying God went before

Contents

1. I Can Meet All Your Needs

Darkness had fallen though it was still early evening. In Burundi, central Africa, which is only about 200 miles from the equator, daylight is usually from six in the morning to six-thirty at night.

A sleek, black car pulled up in front of my house, and a strange man stepped out. For some reason, a cold chill swept over me. As I opened the door to his knock, he handed me a piece of paper with seals and stamps to show it came from the Burundi government. Only a few brief words confronted me: "You are undesirable. According to Article No. so-and-so you must leave the country of Burundi in 48 hours."

The chill settled like a chunk of ice in the pit of my stomach. Leave Burundi? Why? This was my home! Was my missionary service at an end now?

The bearer of the message asked me, "How long have you been in Burundi?" When I replied, "Thirty-five years," he looked at me in amazement and exclaimed, "You must have been born here!"

The next 48 hours were a blur of putting accounts in order, turning work over to others, both Africans and missionaries, grabbing the few things I couldn't part with to take with me on the plane, weeping with African friends who streamed to my home to bid me tearful goodbyes.

Sunday morning came, the day of my departure from Kibuye mission station. Shortly before church time a truck load of soldiers drove in and stopped near my house. My heart sank to my toes! What now? A fellow missionary went to greet them and was told, "We're just here on maneuvers."

Strange! They had never done that before! They fanned out over the mission station armed with guns. The moment the church service was over they began to run through the gardens and across the station, firing their guns into the air, giving me a 21-gun salute in farewell! The congregation was so frightened they hastened home. Yet at that very service, the local government official had come to our church for the first time to publicly thank me for my contribution to his country.

My dad, two brothers and I sit on the old foundation, all that remained after our house was struck by lightning while we were at camp meeting.

The next day on the plane I headed for the United States exhausted physically and emotionally. My mind travelled back across the years to the events that had brought me to this hour.

Born into a Christian home, I was early taught to pray and trust in Jesus. Our family, though poor, was happy. My parents, Duane and Belle Cox, my two brothers, Keith and Bruce, and I lived in the small town of Elsie, Michigan.

One year my mother felt strongly that we must go to camp meeting, though she couldn't see how we could afford it. We children needed clothes, and Dad's suit was shabby. She began to make clothes for us believing that somehow we were going to camp meeting. The situation looked hopeless until just a couple days before time to go. Dad came home from the store where he worked with a big smile on his face.

"What's happened?" asked Mother, a tiny hope rising in her heart.

"The boss just gave me a week off, a bonus of $30, and a new suit!" Dad exclaimed.

What more could one ask? There was great rejoicing. Even my brothers got into the excitement. I was too small to know what was happening.

The week of camp was a blessed time of spiritual victories and growth. Finally, the last Sunday night service came. There were songs and tears of praise as well as regrets at parting from friends. As they began to leave the big tent, my father was handed a message: "Last night your home was destroyed by fire. Lightning appears to have struck in your boys' bed and smoldered for a long time before bursting into flame. By then it was too late to save much of anything."

Shock and sadness swept over my parents until suddenly Mother said, "Praise the Lord! Duane, if we hadn't been at camp meeting, tonight we wouldn't have our boys!" Now they knew the reason for that strong compulsion to be at camp. How wonderfully God had provided, and spared the lives of two little boys! You may be sure those boys got some special

My family in 1922.

hugs that night.

Not long after this we moved to the town of Sandusky, Michigan, where my father ran a bakery. At the age of three, I became desperately ill with pneumonia. The doctor at last told my parents, "Betty Ellen will not live through another night."

Mother went to one room to pray, Dad to another. Each of them, separately, felt God said to them, "If you are willing to give me your only daughter to serve as a missionary, I'll spare her life." Each made that commitment -- but never told me of it till years later.

The next morning the doctor was astonished to see me sitting up in bed begging to get dressed. The fever was gone.

Soon Mother began to sense God pushing her to keep a commitment she had made to him years before. Daughter of a Free Methodist pastor, S. H. Porterfield, she had been saved at an early age. During her teen years, God had clearly called her to the ministry. She accepted the call though it was not easy to be a woman preacher in those days. Now God was holding her to her promise. This required some consecration on Dad's part, too. But both were willing to obey. In due time Mother was appointed to pastor the Free Methodist Church in Harbor Beach, Michigan. Three years later she was appointed to Mayville.

After five years in the ministry, Mother's health failed, and we moved to Spring Arbor. Keith was in high school. Bruce and I attended grade school at Spring Arbor Seminary. Here I met Lorraine Dowley (Whiteman), who was exactly my age. She has been one of my most faithful friends and supporters. Whenever possible, we celebrated our birthdays together. Once she even visited me in Rwanda. What a treat!

During my childhood and teen years, our family had a

Mayville, Michigan, in 1927 just before we moved to Spring Arbor.

hard struggle financially. Yet God always provided for our needs, sometimes in quite miraculous ways. I learned lessons of faith and integrity and "stay-with-it-ness." Needs were often placed before God in family prayers which were a regular part of our home life. Many times we saw those prayers answered.

When Mother's health improved somewhat, her call to preach burned hot in her heart. As she prayed about this, she began to receive calls to hold revival meetings in various places in the Southern and East Michigan conferences. She obeyed God's nudging and leading and many came to Christ through her ministry.

I often felt my mother was a better preacher than many men I heard. There were those who criticized her for being away from her family for two or three weeks at a time, leaving me, a 12-year-old when she began doing this, to cook and care for the home.

Dad probably suffered the most. Sometimes I let the potatoes burn while I played a game of tennis just down the street, or the house filled with soot from an unguarded burner of a kerosene stove. But through this responsibility I learned lessons that I perhaps could not have gotten any other way. Frequently I had the family laundry on the lines to dry before school in the morning. During those years, too, Mother served as interim pastor in Jackson and Albion, Michigan.

While very young, perhaps five years old, I knew I was a sinner and needed to be forgiven. How frequently I quarreled with my brothers and got angry at them, or was proud of an especially pretty dress someone had given me. One evening, after hearing my mother preach, I went forward and asked Jesus to come into my heart. He did! I was so happy I wanted to hug everyone.

When I was 12, I realized I needed the cleansing power of the Holy Spirit. I wanted to serve the Lord, but so often I failed. I was forever having to ask my brothers' forgiveness for getting "mad" at them or my parents' for disobeying them. I was sure there must be a way to be more steady and positive, a way to grow stronger in the Lord. So one day, in the old Spring Arbor stone church, I knelt at the altar and told God he could have all there was of me, that I wanted to be wholly his forever. Soon joy came and thrilled me through and through. The Holy Spirit cleansed me and took full possession of my heart and life. There have been moments of temptation and weakness but I have never wanted to turn away from the One who did so much for me.

A few months later I was in a service where missionary Bessie Reid (later, Kresge) preached a powerful message on commitment for service. Young people were invited to go to the platform to witness their acceptance of this call. A thought flashed through my mind. "What would you do if the Lord called you to go as a missionary?" Quickly, I dismissed the idea, saying to myself, "The Lord would never call me. He knows I can't do anything."

As a child I heard people say, "Betty Ellen can't carry a tune." It was true! I still can't. I was also very shy and fearful of doing anything publicly. How could I be a missionary? But the thought wouldn't go away.

The following year during a missions convention, once more Bessie Reid was the speaker. I was afraid all through the message that she would ask for those who felt called to missionary work to go forward. I thought, "Wouldn't it be awful to say you were called and then never go? If I go forward, people will think, 'How does she think she could ever be a missionary?'" Yet in my heart I feared to disobey God.

What a quandary! True to my fears, the invitation was given. God is so patient with us and so understanding of our motives! Suddenly, a force outside myself lifted me out of my seat and propelled me toward the platform! I knew that wasn't I, but God, and with that realization came the wonderful peace of submission and acceptance.

One would think that such an experience would be proof enough. And it should have been. Yet for several years I wavered, one day gladly saying, "Yes, Lord!" and the next saying, "No, I must be making a mistake. God knows better than to call me. He knows I can't do anything."

At last one day, while I was a college student, the Lord whispered to me, "But you like to learn languages. I can use that." Somehow that settled all my questions. I did, indeed, love to learn languages. I had studied Latin, French, and Greek, and just ate them up. How God meant to use this talent, other than by simply talking to people, I hadn't the slightest idea. But from that day on I had joy and peace in preparing for a missionary career.

Throughout high school and junior college I attended our church school in Spring Arbor, living a sheltered life. For my last two years I was awarded a scholarship to Seattle Pacific College (now University), but that seemed a long way away for this timid girl. When I was given a good offer at Greenville College in Illinois, it seemed right to accept.

My parents were unable to provide much financial assistance though they often sacrificed to help me. However, by my working summers and as much as possible while in school, the Lord enabled me to finish without losing time and owing only $150. Friendships made in those years have been of lasting value, especially with my roommate, Mary Loretta Olmstead (Rose), and one of my teachers, Ruby Dare.

When I arrived in Greenville, wanting to major in Latin, I was directed to Ruby Dare, professor of classical languages and also librarian. I soon realized what a wonderful caring person she was. A short time later when a vacancy occurred on the library staff, I was offered the position. She became not only my teacher and "boss" but also my mentor. When I needed guidance she was quick to sense it and was often there to advise, encourage, and "feel" with me. This continued in the years that followed, mostly by correspondence, but also by visits during my furloughs until the time I returned on furlough in 1968. I looked forward to sharing my concerns with her only to learn that she had just gone to heaven.

Two events left a special impact on me. As an 8th grader in Spring Arbor I found on the campus a good Eversharp pencil. Not knowing the owner, I began to use it. The next year music teacher Mary LaDue offered to give me piano lessons. One day at my lesson she saw the pencil, recognized it as one she had lost, but said nothing. The next day in chapel her husband announced that she had lost a valuable Eversharp and offered a reward to the finder.

Of course, I took the pencil to him, and he promised to give me a dollar. He and I both forgot about it. *Six* years later in Greenville, a professor announced in class one day that each student was to bring a dollar for something. I didn't have five cents, let alone a dollar. I prayed about it and expected it to come in the mail. It didn't. In the meantime the LaDues had transferred to Greenville and ate in the college dining room. The night before my dollar was due, I sat at their table. Suddenly in the middle of the meal, Dr. LaDue looked at me and said, "Betty Ellen, I owe you a dollar!"

"Whatever for?" I asked in astonishment. Then he reminded me of

Ruby Dare, professor of classical languages and librarian, was my mentor at Greenville College the pencil and handed me a dollar. God had saved that dollar for six years to give it to me at the moment of need! This experience has served as a life-long reminder of God's ability to provide for my every need.

While in college I worked in the library as many hours a day as possible in order to earn my way. So studying was often done late at night, and mornings were a rush to get to class. Consequently, my devotional life suffered seriously. I told myself, "The Lord understands. He knows I'd pray if I just had the time." I'm sure he knew, but I was getting very dry.

Finally, the Lord spoke to me about it. I began going to breakfast as early as possible and then slipping into a little prayer room on our floor in the dorm for some time with the Lord before going to class.

How that began to change my walk with him! After about a month of this, one day as I knelt there, I heard the door open. A classmate for whom I'd been earnestly praying entered saying, "Please forgive me for intruding, but I've been watching you come in here daily. Will you pray for me that I'll be saved?" That day she met Christ in a personal way. From that time on throughout my life, prayer and Bible reading have been at the beginning of all my days. I feel I could not have survived without both.

During my senior year I applied to our Missionary Board for missionary service. The reply was: "You are too young to go to the mission field. We advise you to get a job teaching for five years, then we will consider your application."

What a letdown! So I began writing letters of application to everyone I could think of. I majored in Latin thinking that would make it easier to get a job since Latin was still taught in the high schools. But nobody wanted a Latin teacher. Graduation time came with no job in sight.

The day before graduation, the Missionary Secretary came to the campus and asked to interview me. "Would you consider going to Japan immediately?" was his first question. Japan? Now? I couldn't believe it!

But there was a sort of sinking feeling, too. I was interested in more primitive countries where the people didn't have much. Whenever I read of Burundi in central Africa, I longed to go there. But Japan? Yet maybe this was what God wanted. I recalled that in my first letter to the Board, I told them I was willing to go wherever they wanted to send me. So what else could I answer?

"Yes, I'm willing," I replied.

"That's good," he said. "I'd like you to keep yourself free to go just as soon as the Board members make up their minds about you. Some think you are too young at 20, but I don't think you are. Please don't take any kind of a job, even a temporary one."

The very next day I was offered a job teaching in my own home town of Spring Arbor. But

I was 20 and ready for missionary service when I graduated from Greenville College in 1938.

now I couldn't accept it! What if I didn't go to Japan and had turned down the only job I had been offered? I had to turn it down. Late that night I heard a tap on my door. There was Ruby Dare to give me the verse, "Stand still and see the salvation of the Lord." How that helped me in the days that followed!

Graduation over, I was soon on my way back to Spring Arbor, a trip of nearly 500 miles. My brother Keith had come with a trailer to take me and other classmates back home. Trunks and suitcases were loaded into the trailer, and the car was full of young folks. It began to rain very hard, and there was no tarpaulin to cover the trailer. I prayed and prayed that God would make it stop raining so that our things wouldn't get damaged. But the more I prayed the harder it rained! Why didn't God answer my prayer?

When we reached home, no one's things were damaged but mine! I had a cheap cardboard suitcase with a blue lining. The lining had faded all over my clothes and I had no money to buy more. I took the less important things and scrubbed them and used bleach, but the spots were there to stay.

I had just one really good dress, light colored, and it had a big blue spot in front and another in back. Desperately needing the dress, I decided I must at least try to wash it. My mind was still filled with the quandary of what lay ahead for me. As I dipped the dress into the soapy water, I prayed, "Lord, you know I need this dress. Please help me get the spots out."

I lifted it to scrub it, and there were no spots to be seen anywhere! Then it was as if I heard a voice say, "Now, see, I can take care of the rest of your needs just like that." What joy! Now I knew I didn't need to worry about the outcome of these decisions. My heart was at rest.

Now, too, I understood why God had not answered my prayer about the rain. Had it stopped raining, afterward I could have said, "Oh, well, it might have stopped raining whether I prayed or not." But my clean dress was clearly an answer to prayer and gave me full confidence for the future.

The Missionary Secretary had said they would decide

Our entire family was pretty well grown up by 1938. That's me sandwiched between my brothers Keith and Bruce.

quickly whether or not I was old enough to go to Japan. But it took them all summer. At last it was decided -- I was, in fact, too young!

Then I was asked to go as a missionary to the Japanese in California. "We can't offer you a salary if you go there, but you'll have a place to live and something to eat," said the Missionary Secretary. How could I go on that kind of a basis when I still owed $150 on my college education? Yet when I prayed about the offer, I felt God wanted me to go. These were depression years, and my parents had limited resources.

The Missionary Board, hard-pressed for funds, was only able to send me a train ticket from Chicago to Los Angeles. But I didn't live near Chicago! A train trip was necessary and meals would have to be bought during the three-day journey to Los Angeles. I had no money as I had been told not to take even a temporary job.

The Dorr Demaray family from California was visiting our next-door neighbors. They were planning to leave by train for Los Angeles on a certain Monday. It was a perfect opportunity for this timid, small-town girl to make the trip with experienced travellers. Having arranged it with them, I told my friends I would be leaving on Monday. BUT I had no money, nor even a suitcase to pack my clothes in since mine was ruined that rainy night. No one was told of my lack, for I felt this crisis was up to God -- the final test to be sure it was he who was sending me.

Friday came. Just two more days remained until I should leave. That evening during supper a knock came on our door. As I answered, a three-year old neighbor child blurted, "Betty Ellen, d'ya know what? They're havin' a weddin' for you tonight!" She had heard "shower" and that meant wedding to her.

The "shower" was a surprise farewell for me by my Spring Arbor friends. Their gift? You guessed it -- a suitcase! In the pocket of it was a five dollar bill. This would buy my ticket to Chicago! But there was nothing left over for meals en route, yet I knew that God who had provided so much already would not let me go hungry.

A group of friends came to the station to see me off. As I boarded the train, a bundle of letters was pushed into my hand. All were marked with times to be read so they would last for the trip. When I reached my destination, I had bought all my meals and had $40 left over to apply on my college debt. Nearly every letter contained a dollar or two! God does not fail us when we put our trust in him.

2. Learning To Wait

Two happy years passed by as I lived at Redondo Beach, working with children and young people who spoke English. I did, however, learn conversational Japanese so that I could talk with the parents.

The first year I lived with Jennie Tanaka (later Kobayashi, deceased in 1992), a young Japanese woman. She was patient and helpful, introducing me to Japanese culture and people, though she was also very comfortable in American ways. Many were the lessons we learned together. Each of us received a salary of $12.50 per month. Often we had to put much of it into the work in order to keep "Napoleon," our Model A Ford, running. We used Napoleon to gather up children and young people to bring them to our meetings.

Jennie taught me to drive as we went up the mountainous road to our Palos Verde Sunday school. We loved the beauty of the mountains and the nearby ocean. For a special treat we'd each get a 10-cent hamburger and sit on the beach to eat it. Once when our funds and food were gone a Japanese farmer brought us a bushel of cabbages. We ate cabbage three times a day for awhile, fixed in every imaginable way. Another time, when money and food were gone, a Japanese parent whom we seldom saw, but whose children attended our Sunday school, handed us a '"belated Christmas present," a check for $25! That was riches to us!

Eternal rewards were also given to us as children and young people accepted Christ as Savior. Hideo and his sister, Asaki, about nine and ten years old, came from a Buddhist home. One day they came to Sunday school in tears saying, "Our father says we can't come any more. He wants all our family to be Buddhist."

We went to see the father who insisted, "No, they can't go to your

Jennie (Tanaka) Kobayashi and I enjoyed a reunion in March 1990.

Sunday school any more. I want all my family to follow my religion." Then he stopped, sort of surprising himself. "But," he added, "it's a funny thing. I have four children. The other two quarrel and fight and disobey me, but Hideo and Asaki never do. Hey, maybe their going to Sunday school has something to do with that! I guess they can go!"

One night Jennie and I took a car load of young people to a youth meeting about 40 miles away, promising to get them home in good time. We came out of the meeting and discovered that a heavy fog had rolled in from the ocean. We could not see 10 feet beyond the car.

As we drove along slowly, each of us in our hearts began to pray. Suddenly the road was perfectly clear ahead of us. But the fog stood thick at the sides of the road, like a wall. It was as if we were in a white tunnel. The young people were as astonished as we were. They would look ahead and say, "But it'll be foggy up there." Yet it was clear all the way. One fellow said, "You'll see when you get to my place; it'll be foggy. It always is." Again, on the little narrow road to his house, we were still in the white tunnel. All were safely returned to their homes.

"Napoleon," our Model A Ford, transported many children and young people to our meetings.

After a year Jennie married and Mary Chapman (Park) came to work with me. Nearly a year later the Missionary Board decided that I had grown up enough that I could now go to Japan.

Did God really want me in Japan? I wasn't sure. I could only move in the direction God seemed to be leading. So I returned to Michigan and prepared to go to Japan. Soon my trunks were shipped to Seattle from where I was to sail. I was going there by way of California in order to tell my Japanese friends goodbye. Two weeks before my sailing date, the U.S. government issued an order that no women or children could go to the Orient. The year was 1940. War loomed on the horizon.

My friends felt sorry for me. "Twice you've been on the point of going to Japan, and the way has closed. How disappointing!" they said. But I didn't feel that way at all. I had never felt convinced that Japan was where God wanted me, yet I felt I must walk through the doors God opened. Now I was sure it was he who closed them so I was at peace.

My trunks were brought back to California from Seattle, and I was appointed to work in the Japanese church in Stockton. Once more I put my heart into the work, enjoying the youth, and visiting with their parents.

Two of my Japanese friends visited Spring Arbor in April 1940.

Then came Pearl Harbor! As we drove the young people to church that Sunday evening, they crouched down in their seats lest someone see them. What a painful, fearful time the ensuing weeks and months were for them! Orders came for them to go to the Fairgrounds to await transportation to inland relocation camps. They had to sell cars, refrigerators, and furniture for a fraction of their worth. They had to abandon their homes and fields on which they had spent so much labor.

We did all we could to help them while they awaited transfer. Many trunks and boxes of possessions were stored in the church. We shopped for them, searched for things they wanted from their stored goods, visited them daily. We grieved with them over this terrible loss and upheaval until at last their departure time came. As Pastor Oyama told us goodbye, he said, "I have faith in God and I trust America." What a statement of confidence, especially in view of the fact that it was only three years before that he had left Japan to come to America!

What should my next step be? I applied for permission to go to a camp with the Japanese as a missionary. This was denied. Then I applied to go as a teacher, which was also denied, since I did not have a California teacher's certificate. There was nothing left to do but return to Michigan and find employment as a teacher.

In Stockton I boarded in a home where a young lady, Genevieve Strayer, also was living. A friendship soon developed between us, and we moved into a small apartment by ourselves. Gifted in art, she longed to go to college but was unable to do so. Now as I was returning to Michigan, the Lord led and opened doors so that she was able to go with me and attend Spring Arbor College, earning much of her way by teaching art. After completing junior college there she went on to Greenville College and later became a very successful elementary school teacher in Santa Rosa, California. Our friendship has been lifelong and of mutual blessing to us both.

For one year I taught in a high school in Horton, Michigan. Then this school was closed due to lack of teachers. The following year, in Spring Arbor, I taught kindergarten and first grade in the mornings, and a high school and a college class in the afternoons. No one in his right mind would plan a program like that, but God knew I would soon need experience on all these levels, so he just packed it all into one year!

There were times when I complained to the Lord, "You called me to the mission field. Why don't you get me there?" He would patiently remind me, "This is all part of it. It is necessary. This is my plan." Through all of this I was learning that God is completely reliable. I can trust him fully, no matter how difficult the problem.

The Lord paved the way for Genevieve Strayer (right), gifted in art, to attend Spring Arbor College beginning in 1942.

3. Getting There

In 1944 with war still raging, the Missionary Board asked me if I would consider going to Ruanda-Urundi in central Africa (now Rwanda and Burundi). Would I? That was where I had longed to go ever since J. W. Haley had opened work there in 1935! (For that complete story, see *Soul Afire* by Bishop Gerald Bates and *But Thy Right Hand* by J. W. Haley.) Each time I read an article about that new work, my heart thrilled to it. It didn't take long to send an affirmative reply.

Some people tried to discourage me. "You can't make a trip like that in wartime. It's impossible." But I felt that if this was God's plan, he would open the way.

The only neutral ships sailing were Portuguese. It would be necessary to go via Portugal, for which a visa would be needed. One could not make a reservation in advance, but had to go to New York, apply for the visa, and work through an agency to find a ship making the trip.

I left home on September 1 and met Dan and Nancy Wegmueller in New York, with whom I was to travel. We soon moved to New Jersey, to be near Rachel Chilson, a Friends missionary from Burundi. She began to instruct us in the African language while we awaited developments.

In October it looked as if departure might be near so we moved to Philadelphia. The ships had to sail from there. We found lodging with a Free Methodist lady in a first floor apartment below the one occupied by the Free Methodist pastor. We learned that a ship would sail on a Tuesday with about 85 missionaries on board. How excited we were! Surely this was God's plan for us -- if only those Portuguese visas would come! So sure were we that we even took our luggage to the pier. But the ship sailed without us. No visas!

The next day we were told that there would be another ship of a different line on Saturday of the same week. That would be our last chance for months. How we prayed and trusted! We felt the Lord gave us the promise in Isaiah 45:1, "the gates shall not be shut." We were told that in order to make that ship we'd have to have our visas by six p.m. Friday night. But six p.m. came, and there were no visas. Our hearts sank. Were we to be disappointed again? Was it not God's plan for us to go?

Near nine o'clock the telephone in the upstairs apartment began to ring. Our visas! But the pastor and his family were away, and the apartment was locked.

Dan said, "I know how to pick a lock!" A missionary pick a lock? It seemed justified. In moments he had the door open. While the phone still rang he ran up the stairs and lifted the receiver. It was just a member calling his pastor. What a letdown!

Five minutes later the phone rang again. This time it *was* the office calling to tell us that our visas had been granted. Thank the Lord! We were almost too excited to sleep. Early in the morning we went in to New York, got the visas stamped in our passports, and returned to the pier in Philadelphia to board the ship.

Since it was wartime, it was necessary before departure to have a "validation" stamped in the passport. We had these, but they were good for only one month. When the official checked the Wegmuellers' passport, their validation had expired the day before!

Authorization for the validation had to come from a certain woman in the State Department in Washington. But this was Saturday afternoon. All offices were closed. Dan and Nancy begged the official to try to phone that office, but he refused, saying the office was closed. They persisted in pleading with him until he finally made the call just to get them off his back. The particular woman we needed to reach had forgotten something in her office and returned to get it the very moment the phone rang. God's perfect timing! The validation was authorized and we were soon on board ship and ready to begin our long trip.

The voyage across to Europe took 17 days, for we went out in the wake of a hurricane. On reaching Portugal we learned that the ship we missed on Tuesday was with a company that would send no more ships to Africa for three months, and one could not change from the company which issued the ticket. However, the company we travelled with was sending a ship to Africa in two weeks. How beautifully God plans for us!

We arrived at Lobito in Angola on the west coast of Africa. From there we went by train to what is now the Democratic Republic of Congo. As we passed through high mountains on almost frosty mornings, my heart went out to the naked children we saw hugging themselves to keep warm.

Our first Christmas in Africa was spent on board a train.

Travelling by train, bus, and ship, we waited for days between connections. It wasn't until December 29 that we actually set foot on Burundi soil.

How thrilled we were as our ship pulled into port at Uvira across Lake Tanganyika from Bujumbura, Burundi's capital, to be met by Rev.

BURUNDI

ZAIRE

* Kibimba
* **BUJUMBURA**   * Gitega
Muyebe *   * Mweya

* Kibuye

Lake
Tanganyika *   * Bururi   TANZANIA

and Mrs. J. W. Haley! Though there was no one here we'd met before, it felt like reaching home. Burundi's beautiful mountains towered above us. Tomorrow we would drive right up into those high mountains.

4. A Different World

The country of Burundi is tiny, only about the size of
Maryland. Located almost in the center of the continent of
Africa, it is one of the most densely populated countries on
the continent. Though Burundi is close to the equator, the cli-
mate is delightful since much of the country is at an elevation
of 6,000 feet or more. However, it is hot in the capital city,
Bujumbura, located at 2,500 feet altitude on the shore of Lake
Tanganyika.

The scenery is magnificent. From many a vantage point,
on a clear day, one can see tier upon tier of mountains rising
into the deep blue sky. Frequently as I viewed these beauties
of God's creation, I would exclaim, "Oh, Lord, why are you so
good to me? You allow me to serve you in such a beautiful
place!"

Burundi is so small you may have trouble finding it on a
map of Africa. However, no doubt you are better informed
than a nurse's aide I encountered in a hospital in the U. S. She
heard I had been in Africa. "Africa," she pondered, "let me

see, that's somewhere in South America, isn't it?"

Soon the realities of our situation came through to me. Surrounded by friendly people, I longed to talk with them but could say only a few phrases in their language. The Wegmuellers and I were taken to our mission station at Kibuye where Ron and Margaret Collett and Margaret Holton lived. We were warmly welcomed and quickly plunged into language study though there was no textbook. For recreation I taught young Sheila Collett to read.

The houses were nicer than we had expected. One was built with burned bricks, the other with sun-dried bricks which were white-washed. Both had cement floors. The walls were plastered with a mixture of cow manure and sand and painted with a local chalk. Workers carried water in buckets from a nearby spring. Our lighting was by kerosene lamps. We had no refrigeration. (When we finally did get a refrigerator and our cook wanted to take something out of it, he used pot holders -- which he never used to take a pot off the hot stove!)

It was strange to lie in bed at night and hear the hyenas howling, or the beating of drums accompanied by drunken singing. Sometimes it was the heart-rending death wail we listened to. At other times the sound of the singing of hymns came through the night air as some Christian family praised God together. Kibuye is not a town, only a mission station, with scores of African homes on the surrounding hillsides.

One evening after I had been there three months or so, I was alone in our home. The other missionaries had gone away to a convention. We lived under rather primitive conditions and needed to hire helpers. This gave us time for the work we had come to do, and also provided employment for some who otherwise would have had none. Gabo, a young man who was not a Christian, was one such employee.

That evening I began to play some hymns on the hand-wound record player. Gabo, washing dishes in the kitchen, heard the music, came in, and sat down on the floor beside the record player. The Lord whispered to me, "You'd better talk to him about me." The only thing I could think of to say in Kirundi was, "Are you a Christian?" So that is what I asked him even though I knew he wasn't.

He replied, "No, I'm not, but I want to be. That's why I've come in here."

I thought, "Now what do I do?" I said, "Let's pray." We knelt and I began to pray in Kirundi, the language of that country. I prayed as if I had always talked it. Then Gabo prayed and asked God's forgiveness. In a few moments he got up with a joyful face. Then he asked my forgiveness for things he had done -- stolen a little salt, lied about something. I understood every word of it!

The houses were nicer than we expected. This was my first home at Kibuye, Burundi, in 1945.

The next day my housemate, Margaret Holton, returned. I was able to verify that I had understood correctly, for he asked her forgiveness, too. But now I could speak no more of the language than previously. I still had to go through the difficult process of learning it. How able God is to meet our needs!

Many are the errors missionaries make in learning a language so different from English. I once asked the gardener to bring a buffalo (imbogo) when what I really wanted was some lettuce (imboga). A nurse wanted to tell a mother to give her child lots of water (amazi), but instead she told her to give him cow manure (amasi).

To make it even more difficult, the language is tonal. This means that changing the tone or pitch of the voice changes the meaning of the word. The people are very clever to figure out what we mean to say when we butcher their language so badly.

After only two months in Burundi I became quite ill with amoebic dysentery, probably picked up while on my way there. I was treated by our nurse, Margaret Holton, then by a Belgian doctor near our Muyebe station, all to no avail. Finally, our missionaries, the Haleys and the Bergs, took me to a hospital in Kampala, Uganda. After a week or so, the doctor there said I was cured and dismissed me.

But soon after my return the symptoms recurred, more severe than ever. I went to a missionaries' retreat for a time of fellowship, but my condition grew worse. One night the McCreadys and the Bergs came to my tent and said they were going off alone to pray for me. Within an hour my symptoms all disappeared and never returned. God answers prayer! I thank him, too, for fellow missionaries who share our burdens.

One bonus of that experience was the privilege of travelling with the Haleys and the Bergs and seeing some of Africa's most beautiful scenery. This was my first time to see many of the wild animals in a game reserve and we even met a gorilla on the road. Of course, we were in a car!

5. We Know Your Tune

In May, just over four months after our arrival, the Colletts left for their furlough. Margaret had been the principal of the elementary school. Now that responsibility fell on me with my meager preparation. There were about 80 pupils in five grades. The teachers of the classes had only an elementary school education themselves, and there were no textbooks other than a small book containing the four Gospels and two or three of Paul's epistles. Besides doing the work of principal I also taught many of the lessons since the teachers had so little background. It's a wonder the children learned anything at all!

Most of the time I wrote out my lessons word for word in *my* Kirundi. My language teacher, Daniyeli, who knew scarcely any English, would correct my Kirundi lessons for me. He was so patient! Often when he had explained something two or three times he would ask if I understood. Embarrassed to admit that I didn't, I'd say, "Yes."

Looking at me with perception, he'd say, "No, you don't." Then slowly and carefully he'd explain again. Thank the Lord for such a teacher! This situation forced me to learn the language more rapidly.

When the Wegmuellers and I had been at Kibuye just one year, Margaret Holton also went on furlough, leaving us new missionaries to learn on our own. The Lord marvelously came to my help, enabling me to communicate with the Africans far beyond what I had been able to do before.

At that time the school program called for three months of school, then one of vacation, and so on through the year. By this time there were numerous "outschools." These were little buildings out on the hills, sometimes at a great distance from the mission. There a teacher taught reading and writing during the week and held services on Sunday. Most of these teachers had scarcely completed the five years of elementary school. During vacations they would come to the mission, and I would instruct them.

They loved our hymns which had been translated into Kirundi. Often the tunes proved difficult since our scale has eight tones while their music has only a five-tone scale. I thought I needed to teach them how to sing them "right." The way they sang "My hope is built on nothing less" particularly bothered me. While I couldn't sing very well myself, I could teach them with my accordion. After I struggled for some time to help them, one man raised his hand.

"Mademoiselle," he said, "we know your tune, but we like ours better!" End of lesson!

* * * * * * * *

In those early days parents refused to send their girls to school. Girls had to stay at home to carry water, gather firewood, care for younger siblings, and, as they got older, hoe in the garden. I began to visit in the homes of Christians to try to persuade them to send their little girls to school. Various excuses were given for not sending them. "No, we can't spare her. She has to take care of her little brother."

"Girls can't learn anything."

"If she learns to read, she won't want to hoe in the fields anymore. Then no one will want to marry her."

According to this culture, a girl should bring a good dowry to her father. The family of the prospective groom had to give a cow, sometimes more than one.

At last I had a class of eight little girls, all excited about learning to read. Of course, they learned other things, too, especially about Jesus. One day one of the girls, Gakobwa, which means "Little Girl," was missing. The other children said her mother wouldn't let her come. After a couple days Gakobwa was back in school, but in the middle of a lesson her mother burst into the room, grabbed Gakobwa by the arm and pulled her outside. I followed her out to try to reason with her, but she only said, "No, Gakobwa cannot come to your school," and she dragged the crying child away.

A few days later the other children told me that Gakobwa was tied to a post in their house and beaten. I felt I must go see her. After a long walk I reached the grass hut where the family lived. The mother told me Gakobwa had run away. I tried to talk to her lovingly and told her of Jesus' love. The only response I could get was, "No, Gakobwa cannot go to your school."

About two weeks later Gakobwa appeared in class. "Oh," I asked, "has your mother said you can come to school?"

"No," she replied, "but I'm going to come anyway. I must hear more about Jesus."

"Won't your mother beat you?" I asked.

"Yes, she'll beat me, but I can't stay away."

Gakobwa continued to come, and one day she was really saved. Later she worked in a missionary's home. But in her teen years she left and went to the city. In time we learned that she became a prostitute. It seemed so sad when she had paid such a price to learn of Jesus. A number of years later when I was working in the city of Bujumbura, an attractive young woman appeared in our women's sewing class. She waited afterward till the others had gone, then said, "Do you remember me? I'm Gakobwa."

She told of her life of sin, but said, "I want so much to come back to Jesus." We talked and prayed. A few days later she truly repented and found again the joy of the Lord.

* * * * * * * *

After I had been in Burundi six or eight months, I decided I should try to preach in Kirundi. I chose a Sunday when all the other missionaries and most of the African leaders would be away at a special meeting, thus fewer to hear me stumble. At that time the missionaries still did much, though not all, of the preaching. Of course, now it is nearly all done by Africans. Carefully I prepared a message, writing it out word by word. As I sat on the platform waiting to speak, I was handed a note from an outschool teacher in the congregation. He wrote, "I want to preach today." I replied, "So do I! You can preach when I get through."

My laboriously prepared message was delivered in about 10 minutes and I had nothing more to say, leaving ample time for the teacher to preach what he had on his heart.

* * * * * * * *

Early one morning some time after the girls' class began I found a little girl at my back door. She was dressed in a skimpy loincloth and was weeping her heart out.

"What's the matter?" I asked.

Still half-sobbing she replied, "I want to go to school, but I don't have any dress to wear." That was easily remedied. Finding a skirt I could spare, I left the zipper placket unfastened and buttoned the belt button on one shoulder to make an arm-hole, then draped the rest of the belt and skirt under her other arm, leaving the hem much longer on one side than on the other. She was clothed! A bright smile replaced the tears as she happily ran off to school.

What was my surprise a few days later to find the same child crying at my door again. Once more she was clothed in her loincloth!

"What happened to your dress?" I asked.

"The cows ate it," was her tearful response.

In the typical grass hut there is a low partition part way through the house. At night people slept on one side of it and the cows on the other side. She hung her dress on the partition and the cows munched on it. Since I had no more skirts to spare, I took a slip, tied the straps up to make it as short as possible, and clothed her once more.

That little girl, Cimpaye, finished elementary school, then went on to a midwife's training school at another mission station. In due time she returned to work at Kibuye hospital where she served for many years.

6. A Mediocre Job

In those days with untrained teachers and no textbooks, directing a primary school was not easy. The teachers had not learned enough French for it to be useful to them. In fact, I didn't know it very well myself, having had only two years of French in high school. Since Belgium governed Burundi and Rwanda, the official language was French. We were expected to teach it to the children.

I was more interested in providing literature in their native tongue. As soon as I acquired a sufficient knowledge of Kirundi, I began to write arithmetic and geography books for the different grades. My books had little resemblance to the beautifully illustrated volumes used in American schools and no doubt contained some errors in Kirundi, but at least they provided resource material for the teachers and probably enhanced their education.

The African teachers were not the only ones in need of textbooks. Missionaries of several denominations were struggling to learn the language with no book to guide them. When

I had been there about a year, the Alliance of Protestant Missions asked me to write a grammar of the language. I was too ignorant to realize that I wasn't qualified for such a task.

The Alliance also suggested I make copies and distribute them as soon as I had 10 lessons written. This way they wouldn't have to wait until I finished the whole book to get on with their language study.

I wasn't smart enough to know that this process wasn't very wise. For as I wrote I learned more of the language and constantly went back to revise and correct what had already been written. Of course, it was impossible to send all these changes out to those studying the lessons. The corrections would be taken care of when the book was finished and printed in its final form.

However, once the 125 lessons were finished, a missionary of another denomination wanted to be helpful and also to give me a nice surprise. When he returned to the U.S. on furlough, he had 500 copies mimeographed of the original lessons with none of my corrections!

He was proud of what he had done, but I was appalled! I knew how imperfect they were. It took *years* before most of those copies were gone. Only then was I was able to publish a revised edition of the book.

Some years later I was asked to rewrite the book for teaching the language of Kinyarwanda with the help of a national from that country. The language is very similar to Kirundi. Now more than 40 years after the original writing of these books, they are still the language study textbook used by most missionaries in those two countries.

No dictionary existed in which to look up Kirundi words. Therefore, as I learned the language, I wrote the vocabulary words on index cards and filed them alphabetically. Just before I left for my first furlough someone asked if she could copy the words from my cards. Of course, I was willing. When I returned from furlough, to my horror, copies of this book were all over the country as "Betty Ellen's Dictionary!" Once more I knew it was full of imperfections. Besides, I never meant it to be a dictionary. Another job I wasn't very proud to have my name attached to!

But the Lord was teaching me something. I had to consecrate to be willing to do a mediocre job. Oh! I don't mean less than my best! Yet my *best* seemed to turn out imperfect results. But if something is truly needed, an imperfect job is better than a job left undone. Many times the Lord's work suffers because we aren't willing to do the job for fear it will turn out to be less than perfect.

The Lord gave me another lesson along these same lines. During my first term, I was sent to our Muyebe mission station to look after the work while the missionaries normally stationed there were on furlough or sick leave. I spent four months there as the only missionary. At times I went a whole month without seeing another white face or speaking a word of English. There was a short period when I served as mission superintendent, secretary and treasurer. In fact, during most of my years as a missionary, keeping the mission accounts was my responsibility, usually done in the evening hours or whenever I had some "spare" time.

A large church was being built at Muyebe and a Belgian man, with his family, had agreed to move there and complete the building while the other missionaries were away. I went away for a weekend. When I returned I found that the Belgian family had packed up and left, leaving 100 workmen on the job and a kiln full of bricks being burned. The head workman came to me.

"How many days do we fire this brick kiln?" he asked.

These are my bricks!

I hadn't a clue! I knew if it was fired too long the bricks would be black, and if not long enough they'd be mud.

"Don't you know? Can't you remember what you did before?" I questioned.

He didn't. Praying for guidance, I gave him an answer. Then a few days later he was back. "Now how many days do we wait to open the kiln?"

Again I didn't know. And again I prayed for guidance and gave him an answer.

Take a look at my picture of the Muyebe church (which once had the largest membership in the denomination). Look carefully at the tower. You'll see a section where the bricks are a slightly different color from the others. Those are my bricks! And they're still there after more than 50 years! Another case of a mediocre job.

* * * * * * * *

Near the end of my first term Dr. Frank Laubach, with a team of workers including his son Bob, came to Burundi to prepare literacy materials in Kirundi. Probably Dr. Laubach has done more to bring literacy to the nations of the world than any other man. His method has been very successful in many languages.

It was my privilege to serve with the group who worked with Dr. Laubach's team to prepare the lesson materials. Even though each step of the preparation was tested with illiterates, and its usefulness proven before being incorporated into the definitive lessons, I was still a bit skeptical about adults learning to read quickly.

When the lessons were ready, I went back to Kibuye and gathered a group of eight rather old men and women who

"Praise the Lord! I know how to read!" this old man exclaimed after working his way through a whole chart prepared by Dr. Frank Laubach and his team.

wanted to learn to read. It was exciting and amazing to watch their progress and reaction. One old man would screw up his face to figure out the letters and pictures. When he had somewhat stumblingly read a whole chart his face would burst into sunshine as he exclaimed, "Praise the Lord! I know how to read!"

A young man of about 20, Emanuweli, hearing of this class, came to me and said, "Won't you teach me to read?" He had never gone to school. I agreed. In a remarkably short time he had mastered the lessons. We were then writing "Stories of Jesus" according to the Laubach method. As fast as I'd get a story written and typed, I'd give him a copy. He would come back the next day reading it.

One day as he came, Emanuweli waved his paper at me and said, "Is this really true? It says a woman was sick and no one could help her, but she came to Jesus and just touched the hem of his garment and she was well. Is that really true?" I assured him it was.

"Is that our Jesus?" he asked. "Could he do things like that today?"

"Yes," I affirmed. "That is our Jesus, and he can do just as great things today."

He ran outside with his paper to a group of his friends standing there. He shouted, "Hey, fellows, listen to the most wonderful thing you ever heard of!" Briefly he told the story, then exclaimed, "And fellows, that's our Jesus! He can still do things like that!"

I'm sure Emanuweli had heard sermons about that story, but that day he read it for himself and it came alive. That is one of the reasons I got involved in writing and translating books into their language.

Another thing that pushed me into literature work was

the evident hunger for books in those who learned to read. I like books, and I had two bookcases full of them in my living room. Sometimes an African visiting in my home would carefully look over all those books, then say, "Have you read all these books?"

"Yes," I'd reply.

Then he'd say, "You must be very wise! But isn't there even one of them in my language?" There were none. My heart burned to help satisfy that hunger. At the end of my first term, I could easily hold in one hand all the literature that existed in the Kirundi language.

From this time on, during the years I was a teacher, most of my free time was spent producing literature of one sort or

I'm holding all the Kirundi literature that existed in 1950.

another. One dear lady in America heard of our great need for books and longed to help. She wrote, "If you'll just send me an English-Kirundi dictionary, I could translate some books for you." Unfortunately, translating isn't that simple.

7. Sorrow -- And Joy

Other new missionaries came to join us at Kibuye. The Wegmuellers went to Kibogora in Rwanda and Allen and Lillian Bilderback came to replace them. The medical work was growing and a hospital was being built, so Dr. Esther Kuhn came to join us. Elizabeth Van Sickle and Berdina Beckwith, both nurses, also came to Kibuye. Elizabeth was a teacher as well as a nurse. Though my knowledge of the language was still limited, it became my responsibility to teach it to the new missionaries.

Throughout the rest of my years on the mission field I was seldom without a language student. For many missionaries, learning a new language is one of the hardest things they have to face. For others it is a delight. One student, whenever he encountered some new difficult point of grammar, acted as if I had invented that particular item just to make life difficult for him!

Berdina lived with me, and Dr. Kuhn and Elizabeth shared another small house. Berdina was doing well with the language and was liked by the Africans. Suddenly she was taken ill with appendicitis. Since Dr. Kuhn was not a surgeon, she took her to an Anglican hospital where there was a surgeon. For several days Berdina seemed to get along all right, then quite unexpectedly she worsened and died. It was concluded that her death was caused by chloroform used for the anesthetic in the surgery.

It was hard to believe she was really gone, that one so young and with such a promising future before her was taken after only two years as a missionary. Yet in our sorrow we knew we could trust the all-wise, all-loving plans of our heavenly Father.

Within three weeks of her death I was to leave for my first furlough. Now I not only had to pack away all my things, but also decide which of Berdina's things should be brought home to her family, and which should be disposed of in Burundi.

Berdina Beckwith died after only two years in Burundi.

During my last year before furlough I developed a stomach ulcer so my term was cut to only six years instead of the seven I anticipated. Later the Missionary Board reduced the length of a term to five years and eventually to four.

Facing the deputation ministry expected of furloughing missionaries floored me. (Deputation is the visitation to various churches across the country to present the cause of missions.) What did I have to say that people would want to listen to? The responsibility looked impossible. As I prayed about it the Lord gave me words he long ago gave to Jeremiah: "Be not afraid of their faces, for I am with thee . . . . Behold I have put my words in thy mouth" (Jer. 1:8,9). With that I knew the Lord would enable me.

Thus my travels in 1950-51 took me all across the United States, east and west, while my home base was in Elsie, Michigan, with my parents. For the most part I was given a wonderful reception. People were very kind, but one place was an exception. I arrived by train and was met by the pastor whose first words, after introducing himself, were: "I want you to know I don't believe in missions. It wasn't my idea to have this service." Then he took me to the home of a member who lived next door to the church.

Later he joined us in that home for the evening meal. "I have a nephew who wants to be a missionary," he said, "but I'd rather he'd go into *any* profession other than that. What do you do out there anyway, sit and twiddle your thumbs?"

I told him simply of my call and a little of what God had done in Burundi. He seemed to soften a bit. Then it started to rain. "Oh," he said, "there's no use going over to the church at all. Our people don't come when it rains."

"Well," I replied, "I think I'll go over anyway. I've already set up my projector and display." I went, and so did he, and so did 40 or 50 other people! The Lord gave us a good service. A young woman, who had only come to drive a group of singers and who never attended church, was clearly saved as we conversed and prayed after the service. God has his recompense for us that more than makes up for any problems we encounter.

This furlough, which covered two years, included a year in Belgium. At that time Burundi and Rwanda were governed by Belgium as a trusteeship under the United Nations. Missionaries engaged in medical or educational work were required to spend a year studying French and other courses provided by the Belgian government. I had not been able to do this previous to my first term due to the war.

In the United States I met Evelyn Rupert (now Heath) who was appointed to Burundi as a teacher. So we went together by ship to Belgium. It was a year of hard study but also some fun times. We took various trips to see interesting places in Belgium and surrounding countries. We lived with a Belgian family and were immersed in the French language.

During that year I also had the experience of a stay in a Belgian hospital. I had somehow contracted typhoid fever. The hospital authorities didn't want to treat me. They didn't want to believe there could be any typhoid in Brussels. But they refused to release me until I had a negative blood test. After a week of this impasse, though still with a positive test, I was released -- I believe in answer to prayer. Treatment by a private doctor was eventually successful.

8. Faith That Moves Mountains

How happy Evelyn and I were to finally arrive in Burundi in October 1952! For her it was the beginning of her missionary career. For me it was a new beginning in a new location.

Since 1949 the Belgian government subsidized our Protestant schools, a policy they had followed for Catholic schools for a long time. But in order to receive these benefits our African teachers had to have more training. Consequently, the Alliance of Protestant Missions started a high school level teacher training school at a Friends (Quaker) mission station, Kibimba. The participating missions were expected to provide the teachers for this school. I was sent as the Free Methodist member of the staff. Kibimba was about a two-hour drive from Kibuye where I spent my first term.

Now I had the opportunity to put to work the French I had been acquiring the previous year. All courses had to be taught in French. Believe me, it wasn't easy! Students having passed a national examination were assigned to the school by the government. They came from all the Protestant churches.

Here was a wonderful opportunity to help many young men (girls were not admitted till several years later), not only to develop intellectually, but to get a strong spiritual foundation. Many of the students were not yet saved when they arrived.

Immediately I urged my friends and correspondents to pray for our students. One Sunday, at the close of a Sunday school lesson which seemed quite ordinary, six students spontaneously said they wanted to repent and be saved. We prayed for them, and their faces showed that a transformation had taken place. A few weeks later, a letter from Spring Arbor, Michigan, told of a Friday noon fast prayer meeting at which earnest prayer was offered for our Kibimba students. It was the Friday just preceding that particular Sunday!

"The Lord wants you to be his donkey!" Rather a shocking statement! Benyamini, an evangelist, was preaching to our students. His text was the story of Jesus sending his disciples for the donkey on which he was to go into Jerusalem. "There was the donkey, perfectly strong and able to carry, but useless because he was tied up. Going his little round on his rope, he had cleaned up the grass there. Sometimes he wanted more or was thirsty, but he was tied. He never did any work because he was tied. Then the disciples untied him, and away he went to carry Jesus wherever he wanted to go. Are you the Lord's donkey? Are you tied up by sin, pride, selfishness, or something else, going your little round, doing nothing for Jesus? Let him untie you, then go, carry him on your back wherever he wants his message to go."

The Lord preceded the revival meetings where Benyamini was preaching. About a week earlier at the end of a Bible lesson, a student suddenly burst into weeping. He fell on his knees asking others to pray for him. He was the leader of some trouble among the students a few months before. He was proud and hard, hating the dormitory supervisor,

Samweli. As he rose and asked for forgiveness, he turned to the one he hated saying, "Samweli, I'm going to love you and I'll do what you tell me. The Lord's going to help me."

Benyamini was a man wholly committed to Jesus. His conversation centered on Jesus, everywhere and always. In the midst of talking about something else, he would suddenly laugh and say, "Isn't our Jesus wonderful? Why, he can do anything!" Nearly all the students received definite help during those few days of meetings. Even the atmosphere at the school changed.

After a year on the staff of this school I became the director. This meant handling academic matters, seeing that there was food for all the students, and making sure the dormitories were properly managed. I also had to settle any problems with the students and teachers and deal with the government in all affairs pertaining to the school. It seemed a bit incongruous for me to be directing a boys' school, but there was no one else to do it.

Naturally, as in any school situation, there were lots of interesting answers to exam questions. On a hygiene test in answer to the question, "What is the function of the blood?" a student wrote, "To wash the bones." English was taught as a third language (after Kirundi and French). On an English test in reply to the question, "What do you do every morning?" one said, "Every morning I get on my bed and I wash my front." (The French word for "face" is "front.")

I've learned that being a missionary involves doing many jobs for which one has no training. I even delivered a baby once while at Kibimba while someone read to me out of a book what to do! Nature took its course, it was a normal delivery, and everything turned out all right.

At this school we had a dorm manager who looked after

the daily details of food buying, as well as overseeing the dining department and the work program of the students. Samweli came to us with his wife, Yudita, from another mission station some distance away. Yudita was lonely, for she had not made many friends yet in this new location, and she was pregnant. I tried to be friendly to her whenever we met, but being very busy, I hadn't gone out of my way to visit her.

One unusually busy morning, Samweli came to me and begged me, "Yudita has run away. Please take me in your car to try to find her." I couldn't refuse. He was sure she must have gone to a witch doctor. As we searched everywhere he could think of, my conscience began to trouble me. I thought, "When have I ever tried to be a real friend to Yudita? When have I encouraged her in the Lord?" The hymn by Lucy R. Mayer went through my mind:

He was not willing that any should perish.
Am I His follower, and can I live
Longer at ease with a soul going downward,
Lost for the lack of the help I might give?

As we drove along, I prayed and promised the Lord that if he would bring Yudita home I'd do my best to become her friend. We returned from our search without her.

Two days later Yudita was back. Although it was another busy day, I put everything aside and went to see her. I began by asking her to forgive me for not taking time for her. This melted her heart, and she poured out her story. In Burundi a mother carries her baby on her back, tied on usually with a goat skin. This skin is so important that it is called by the same name as the placenta. They believed that if this skin should get torn or damaged, the next baby would die. Her skin had gotten torn, and she was soon to have a baby. In their beliefs only a witch doctor could help in such a situation. When she had discussed this with her husband, he had only scolded her for entertaining such thoughts.

I reminded her of Jesus' love, that he cares about everything that happens to us, and that his power is greater than any other. Then we prayed together, mingling our tears. She asked God to forgive her doubts. I asked forgiveness for neglecting a friend. Soon she arose with a smile shining through her tears, saying, "I'm only going to trust Jesus now." In due time Yudita delivered a healthy baby. And I learned an important lesson.

* * * * * * * *

Near Kibimba lived an old blind lady who dearly loved the Lord. Visiting her was a source of inspiration. Though she didn't have anyone to help her regularly, she was always joyful. Once when we visited we gave her a piece of soap, an item usually treasured, but she said, "Oh, thank you, but I don't need it. Jesus washed me with a much better soap." On another occasion she was given a dress. Her response was, "Thank you, but I'll not be here long to wear it. Soon I'll have a beautiful white one in heaven when I'm with Jesus." I'm sure she's wearing that white one now.

Whether at Kibimba or elsewhere, sometimes the differences between our American ways and the African culture were hard for Africans to understand. For us there was often the tension of wanting to be as close to the nationals as possible, yet we felt the need to maintain a healthful lifestyle that could be an example for them to follow. Our homes were modest and simple, made of local materials, but they were luxurious in the eyes of people who lived in small, dark grass houses. By contrast to those whose annual income was under

$100, we were very rich indeed. One day an African man came to me and said, "You know, I don't think you white people love your children like we do."

This was a surprise to me! I heard new missionaries say of Africans, "If these people really loved their children, they'd know instinctively to take better care of them." There was much illness among the children and the infant mortality rate was very high.

I replied, "Why do you say that?"

He answered, "Why! If we had a child that went away for even a year, we'd get so lonesome we couldn't stand it. We'd just cry. But you come here and stay all these years! It can't be your parents love you very much."

"Oh, but they do love me just as much as you love your children," I answered. "They get lonesome. Sometimes they cry. But they love the Lord Jesus, and they love you, even though they've never seen you, so they *want* me to come here."

The old man's eyes filled with tears, and he said, "We don't have that kind of love in our country."

The traditional religion of Burundi is animism, a belief that inanimate objects such as trees and rocks are inhabited by spirits, both good and bad. The *Barundi* (people of Burundi) believe there is only one God who created the world and everything in it. He is good, but no longer pays any attention to people. They believe that after creation an evil one came along and tried to destroy the good that God had done, so he brought death and sickness and crop failure and everything that is bad into the world. They worship, not God but the evil one, in an attempt to satisfy him so he won't bring these bad things to them.

The Barundi also believe that death first came into the

world through a woman. Another belief is that on rare occasions God shows himself to people in the visible form of a pure white lamb! So the biblical words "Behold the Lamb of God" do not surprise them.

An interesting practice must surely have come down to them somehow from Old Testament times, that of a scapegoat. When an epidemic or other calamity struck the country, the elders would take a goat, place their hands on its head, describe in detail the calamity and then say, "Now go, take all of these troubles with you." One man would then lead the goat off to an uninhabited area and leave it. Consequently, no one wanted to accept a stray goat into their flock, lest it be a scapegoat bringing trouble.

* * * * * * * *

Earthquakes are not uncommon in Burundi though they usually don't do a great deal of serious damage. One Sunday afternoon I was writing a letter expressing my concern that people seemed slow to turn from their sins. I had just written, "I wish the Lord would shake some of these people loose . . ." when the table, the house, and the ground began shaking violently! I ran outside as did my missionary neighbors. As we stood out in the open, I laughingly told them what I had just written. One of them remarked, "You really had faith that moved mountains, didn't you?"

9. Oh Joy! I'll See Jesus!

Once again a health problem necessitated my leaving the field a year early. This time I was having severe head pains that appeared rather serious. The Lord undertook for my physical need working through a Christian doctor. Before long I was ready for the usual deputation ministry. Many people were a blessing and inspiration to me as I travelled from place to place. Also, furlough time always helped me get a new perspective on my ministry, almost like observing someone else.

Once, arriving at a church after the service began, I waited in the foyer with quite a group of people. One woman, on recognizing me, whispered loudly to her five-year old son, "That's the missionary." The little fellow looked me up and down, then said disgustedly, "Naw, that ain't no missionary!" I wondered what he thought I should look like.

While I was on this furlough with my parents in Elsie, Michigan, my mother had a light stroke which caused her to lose the sight of one eye. The doctor found a cataract forming on her good eye. At that time cataract surgery was not as simple as it is now, and not always successful. I suggested that perhaps I should stay home to care for her if she lost her sight altogether. Mother assured me that God would take care of her. Indeed he did! In the remaining five years of her life, the cataract never advanced any further.

I fully expected to return to Kibimba to continue my teaching there. Imagine my surprise to be informed, about two weeks before leaving for Burundi, that I was appointed to Bujumbura, the capital. I was to be principal of our new elementary school. Missionaries Oddvar and Peace Berg and Paul and Estelle Orcutt had begun our Free Methodist work there the year before.

I had gone to the capital many times to shop or do business. It was *hot* there, as the elevation was only 2,500 feet instead of the 6,000 feet of most of the rest of the country. When business was done and we were on the way up the mountain, as we'd hit cooler temperatures, with a sigh of relief I'd exclaim, "Thank the Lord, he didn't send me to work in Bujumbura!" Now he had!

A new section of the city was built by the government especially to house "white-collar" African workers. In this section the government gave our mission a residence building comprising four apartments and an elementary school complex with 18 classrooms, plus offices. They promised to build a church and youth center, a promise they fulfilled later.

The year before, Estelle started the school with a few classes. Now we had to fill these 18 classes. If we couldn't, the government threatened to take away from us at least some of the buildings. With fear and trembling and much time spent seeking the Lord's help, I undertook this awesome task. In due time the classes filled and enough teachers were found.

Children of 30 different tribes came to our school, many

not knowing either Kirundi or French. Of necessity, I had to learn Swahili, an inter-tribal trade language, in order to communicate, especially with the parents. Classes had to be taught in French from grade one on up.

The following year, due to some changes in staff, we were short one teacher. School would open in a month. A young man, Frederic, came to apply for the job. He was a graduate of Kibimba, but while there he had vowed never to become a Christian, though I didn't know that at the time. I asked him, "Are you a Christian?" We had a policy to hire only Christian teachers.

Quite frankly he replied, "No, I'm not."

I thought how glibly many would have said, "Yes," in order to get the job. "Then," I said, "I'm afraid we can't use you because one of our purposes is to win children to Christ. An unsaved man couldn't do that."

Yet he seemed so fine, I couldn't get him out of my mind. Two weeks later he came back. In spite of my policy I felt strangely impressed to hire him so I took the matter to the church school committee. They agreed he should be hired.

Many times I lifted my heart to God in prayer for Frederic. Two weeks after school started he came to my office one afternoon. Without delay he said, "I want to be saved. Will you pray for me now?" Together we prayed and God met Frederic's need. Two or three months later, children in his class began to seek the Lord. How radiant he was when he came to tell me that nine of them had found Jesus!

After we finished registering pupils for the school year, a mother with her three young children came to enroll them. She said, "I started my children in another school but they came home crying. They want to go to the school where they sing." She hummed a couple lines of "Jesus loves me" to indicate the type of singing she was interested in. Of course, I couldn't turn away a request like that, though all the classes were full!

One of the teachers, in conducting morning devotions in his class, asked for a child to volunteer to pray. After some time of silence, finally a child said, "Teacher, we don't know how to pray. We've never prayed before." Upon inquiry the teacher found that only one pupil in his class had ever prayed before. At first he was discouraged. Then he recognized that this was a marvelous opportunity and challenge.

In the sixth grade class was a boy, Shabani, who was always making trouble. Two or three times his teacher had come to me asking that we expel him. Each time I said, "Let's be patient with him a little longer and pray for him more." One morning in class Shabani raised his hand. Being given permission to speak, he said, "I've been such a bad boy. I've quarreled and fought, stolen books, and other things. I want Jesus to forgive me. Here are some of the books I took, and I'll try to find the others." His teacher prayed for him and Shabani was a changed boy.

At the same time in a first grade class, almost the same thing happened, only in this case the child had stolen money. The next morning, in almost every class, the routine Bible lesson turned into an altar service, with many children coming to Jesus. The teachers were amazed and were quite unprepared for this movement. Repentance and restitution were made, stolen articles returned, forgiveness asked for fighting and hatred. At recess times and noon hours little groups of children were clustered in various places, singing hymns and testifying.

A few days later, these children from pagan homes asked their teacher, "Couldn't we be giving something to Jesus since he's done so much for us?" They'd never heard of offerings in church! The whole class decided they wanted to do that, so they began to bring their francs, eggs, bananas -- whatever they could find. When the teacher told another about the children's giving, the other remarked, "Well, if the gospel does that to children, I guess we don't need to fear for the future of the church here!"

Among the children in the school were two little Muslim brothers. When they entered this Protestant school their father strictly warned them, "Learn all you can of their wisdom but you are to have nothing to do with their religion!" They obeyed up until the day the Holy Spirit powerfully moved among the children.

That day the older of the two repented of his sins and received the Lord Jesus as his Savior. At home that night the younger brother tattled on him. When the father heard it he was very angry and beat the child severely, threatening him, "Now, leave their religion alone! If you don't, I'll take you out of school."

In spite of these threats, the joy in his heart was so great that he couldn't give up. The younger boy watched with wonder the change that had come over his big brother. There was no more lying, no more bullying him, no more quarreling.

Soon the younger lad decided that it was even worth a beating to have Jesus come into his heart. He repented and found the same joy. The boys decided they must go together and tell their father all about it and take whatever consequences there might be. As they feared, their father was furious, whipped them, and repeated the earlier threat.

The next morning the boys expected to be told they could not go to school, but they got ready as usual, and not a word was said. The father, watching the changed lives of his children, admitted that his religion had never done so much for him, so he interfered no more.

* * * * * * * * *

These were years when the word "independence" was beginning to float around. Racial feelings were becoming rather strong. People were tense, expecting something to happen any day.

In neighboring Rwanda the Hutu people, long held in subjection by the minority Tutsis, finally revolted. Thousands of Tutsis were slaughtered or maimed, as were their cattle. Many thousands more fled to Burundi, Tanzania, and Congo. From that time on the Hutu held power in Rwanda until 1994. Reports of these events aggravated the mounting tensions in Burundi. A slight rumor would swell to great proportions and often have dire consequences as people were moved by emotion rather than by reason.

One day at a government dispensary near our school a long line of people waited for treatment. A national nurse, treating children for worms, made a mistake and administered the wrong medicine. In a little while the group of children went into convulsions. The waiting crowd began to throw rocks and bottles, smashing windows and shouting, "The white people are killing our children!" But there were no white people around. The thoroughly frightened nurse hastily called the city hospital for help for the stricken children. Ambulances set out with stomach pumps and other helps. Though it was only a distance of three miles, by the time they arrived the mob was acting far beyond reason and tried to overturn and destroy the vehicles. The help that could have saved those lives never got there, and nine little children needlessly died.

By that time frenzied parents all over the city heard the

cry, "The white people are killing our children." Descending on the schools everywhere, parents dragged their children out doors and windows in utter terror and panic. Most of them did not really know what had happened, only that their children were supposedly in danger. It was a long while before most of the children were back in school again.

On another occasion an attempt was made to give BCG shots to prevent TB, which is very prevalent. Rumors were started that this was an attempt to sterilize the people and so eventually wipe out the black people. It was impossible to continue the immunizations.

* * * * * * * *

An important event for Burundi in 1960 was the Billy Graham crusade in Bujumbura. Much preparation went into this with interdenominational prayer meetings, training classes, and negotiations with the government for permission for the meetings. The times were tense as neighboring Congo was being granted independence, and rumors were flying related to Burundi's own independence.

Permission was initially given to use the stadium. Less than a month before the announced date of the crusade the government withdrew that permission. Then the government said the meetings could not be held at all for fear of political trouble. An appeal was made to reconsider the decision but it was still denied just eight days before the scheduled date. A couple days later they agreed that the meetings could be held but only in a covered building -- yet there was none large enough in the city. The planning committee decided to use three separate buildings with telephone relays: the Free Methodist church, a government auditorium, and a high school auditorium.

The great day came, a Sunday morning, and so did the crowds. There were about 3,500 in the FM church and 1,000 or more in each of the other locations. Roy Gustafson was the preacher with interpretation into Kirundi. He gave a powerful salvation message and the sound system worked well in all three places. Police patrolled all around the sites. There were about 500 seekers in our church plus many in many in the other buildings.

Afternoon and evening services were held with good attendance and response. This interest continued Monday and Tuesday until, on Wednesday, the entire Billy Graham team arrived. At the last minute the government gave permission for outdoor meetings in a big field adjoining the Danish Baptist headquarters -- and it rained! I was deeply moved as I sat with at least 3,000 people in the rain listening to Cliff Barrows preach. There were many seekers. Satan was doing his best to hinder, but God worked powerfully anyway. That evening (with interpretation) Billy Graham spoke to a French-speaking congregation in the government building. There were at least 300 Belgians and many educated Africans. Quite a number raised their hands to indicate their desire to follow Christ. Perhaps for some it was the first evangelical message they had heard.

Finally on Thursday morning a service was held in the field (the rain had stopped) with 4,000-5,000 present. Mr. Riggs preached. In the afternoon Billy Graham addressed the crowd of 6,000 or so. The message was clear and Spirit-anointed, and crowds responded.

There was a terrific jam of cars as the location wasn't really adequate. Frank Adamson purposely parked at the far outside edge, and I rode with him to get home early to serve many guests. As we were just ready to leave, along came Billy

Graham and three team members on foot. They were invited to evening dinner with the governor and the car they came in was deep in the middle of the traffic jam.

They told us their plight. Of course, we were delighted to assist. It was my privilege to sit next to the evangelist himself for the three or four miles to the hotel. I was impressed with how ordinary, yet poised, he seemed. Only eternity will reveal the impact of those few days that Billy Graham and his team spent in that tiny country in the center of Africa.

* * * * * * * *

For some time while I was working in Bujumbura, I had been having severe dizzy spells and occasional chest pain. But I was too young for the symptoms to be considered heart trouble. Then one day the pain and dizziness were so severe that I was taken to the Bujumbura hospital.

The next morning the doctor concluded it was a heart attack and ordered an injection of heparin. Moments after the nurse left the room after giving the injection, I knew something was desperately wrong. By the time the nurse was called back, and then the doctor, I could not speak. I had no pulse and no blood pressure, and soon lost consciousness. Four or five hours later, the voice of the nurse saying, "Breathe, breathe," roused me.

The doctor returned to see me after I was nearly back to normal. He said, "I never thought I'd see you breathe again."

The next day the Catholic nurse asked, "Did you know you were dying?"

"I thought maybe I was," I replied.

"Were you afraid?" she asked.

As I thought back to those last moments of consciousness, I recalled just two thoughts that had flashed through my mind: "Oh joy! I'm going to be with Jesus!" and "But who's going to do my work?" The people among whom I lived had a terrible fear of death. Now I could testify to them, "I came face to face with death and felt only joy."

A few weeks later a letter came from Mary Loretta Rose. She asked, "On such and such a date I felt a special urge to pray for you. What was your need?" It was the very day of my brush with death. Thank God for faithful pray-ers!

With national independence approaching, it was important to have nationals prepared to assume responsibility, not only for teaching in the schools, but also for handling administration. A great deal of unrest existed among the teachers as well as in the general population. Though the school was government subsidized and the teachers' salaries set and paid by the government, the funds still passed through my hands so I was accused of not paying them enough.

The teachers sent their own representatives to inquire about their salaries at the Educational Office and even to the government Finance Office to look at the official records of subsidies paid, all of which corroborated the accuracy of our handling of the funds. Yet they still insisted that I was withholding some of what they should have. Two or three ringleaders practically compelled all the other teachers to join them in their vigorous protests.

These attitudes provoked a very stressful time with seemingly no way to bring peace and reconciliation. Even the church's school board was unable to get the teachers to see reason. Undoubtedly this was largely due to the anti-white sentiment that prevailed in the country as it moved toward independence from Belgium. At the end of the school year, 12 of our best qualified teachers resigned. I was not really sorry to see them go, only sorry that we were unable to reach an amicable solution.

A postscript should be added here. Six or seven years later, the man who had been one of the leaders in stirring up this conflict said to me, "Miss Cox, if it hadn't been for you, the Free Methodist church would have nothing in Bujumbura today." I recognized this statement was not really true but sensed this was the closest he could come to apologizing and acknowledging that he and the others had done wrong. The work in Bujumbura was then flourishing.

We secured enough teachers for the next school year and Samweli (not the man mentioned in Chapter Eight) was in training to be director, or principal, of the school. One of the few who stayed with us, he showed a beautiful spirit and an aptitude for administration.

At this time, in addition to my other responsibilities, I was asked to teach Kirundi to the U. S. ambassador, his wife, and some of the staff members in the city. A lasting friendship developed with them that continues to this day, though the ones I taught were in Burundi only two years.

During the 1960s the Belgian Congo (now Democratic Republic of Congo) became independent. Since Ruanda-Urundi was also under the Belgian government, events in the Congo brought serious tensions in Burundi. When fighting endangered the lives of Europeans, most missionaries had to flee. Many of them, especially those in eastern Congo, came to Burundi and sought lodging with us. At one time we had more than 30 missionary refugees, mostly Methodists, staying in our three rather small apartments. They came with frighten-ing accounts of harassment and narrow escapes which made us wonder what lay ahead for us.

With all these stresses, I sometimes felt the same as Anania, our Bujumbura pastor. Once when he was preaching he said, "Sometimes I think I want to go to be a pastor in the country (he'd been pastor in the city for many years), where I could have gardens and earn a little money on the side. Then sometimes I want to go back to my own tribe in the Congo. But I come to conference and hear the appointments, and the Bishop says, 'Bujumbura -- Anania Emedi.' My heart sinks. Back to the city again! Then God says, 'If you forsake my sheep and lambs there in the city and they perish, what will you say when you stand before me?' So once again I go back with joy to my work in the city -- to the dust, the heat, the many guests (seldom fewer than 25 at his table), the wickedness -- with the presence of the Holy Spirit, to seek the lost sheep and pasture the ones God has given me."

The constant presence of guests was an important aspect of our work in the capital. Missionaries of all denominations coming to the city to do business often stayed with us. Gerald and Marlene Bates, living next door, and I often each served more than 100 guest meals every month. Cooking is not my speciality so I was glad when I had a good African cook. At times when I was in the throes of teaching a new cook, it took more time and effort to be a gracious hostess. Yet the fun and fellowship with these fellow-workers were rewarding, too.

By the beginning of the 1961-62 school year Samweli was able to handle more responsibility and was given full charge. I was nearby to help if he needed it. This freed me to give nearly full-time to the literature ministry, a work I had been longing to do.

10. This Book Works

What a joy it was to concentrate my efforts on the most important literature there is -- the Bible! I recalled a time a few years earlier when the entire Bible was first printed in the language of Rwanda, a language enough like Kirundi that the Barundi can understand it. An African pastor, speaking to his congregation with his new Rwanda Bible in his hands, said, "For the first time in my life I hold in my hands the whole Word of God in a language I can understand. I am terrified to think what a responsibility that means to us Christians. Either it is life, more precious than gold, more precious than one's family, his house, or the greatest honor one could have -- or it is death!" Such a profound thought!

Most of the translation of the Bible into Kirundi had previously been done by Rosemary Guillebaud, an English missionary. Over a period of about 15 years she worked with a team of two Barundi. When they finished one book of the Bible they distributed copies to various people who checked the book for accuracy.

Strange problems occur in translating to another language. One of the early passages translated was the Lord's Prayer. "Our Father"(*data* in Kirundi) can mean either "our father" or "my father." Wanting to make sure people understood it to be "our father," the translator put with it the word *wacu*, which means "our." He did not realize that the combination *data wacu* changed the meaning and made it say "my uncle." So for a time people prayed, "My uncle who is in heaven."

Discovering that error and wanting to keep the precious thought that calling the same one "our Father" makes us brothers and sisters, they settled for "Father of us all."

Think of the verse "Behold I stand at the door and knock." At that time the Barundi all lived in grass houses. No one "knocked" at a door, so there is no word for that. Instead, they stood outside and coughed or cleared their throat. So the verse in their language says, "Behold I stand outside and cough."

A significant point in the translation was a definitive decision about the word to be used for "God." Sometime in the 1950s a language committee with a representative of the Bible Society discussed this matter. The Kirundi *Imana* had been used from the beginning, and most of the concepts associated with it were not contrary to Christian doctrine.

However, the same word was also used for "fate" and even for "luck." It was feared some other non-Christian idea might be attached to it as well. Some suggested using the Hebrew word, others the Swahili (which the Catholics used), but in the end it was decided to keep the Kirundi word *Imana*. Years later, following independence, an African in his preaching said, "Some people say that Christianity is the white man's religion, not ours. But that isn't so. The same *Imana* that our ancestors believed in and talked about is the *Imana* of

Christianity." The decision to use this particular word was made under God's guidance long before and enabled the people to grasp that Christianity belongs to the Barundi and is not imposed by foreigners.

My share of the work was not translating. I was asked to type almost the entire manuscript of the Bible. They wanted this to be read in its entirety by a large committee of Barundi from various parts of the country. This would ensure that the translation was accurate and acceptable in all areas. I was asked to type it on stencils and mimeograph it. This project took several months and 1,700 stencils.

One hot afternoon I stood by an open window running the mimeograph. There had been troubles and massacres in Rwanda. Thousands of refugees had fled to Bujumbura and were being temporarily housed nearby. Streams of them walked by on a path near the window where I worked.

One curious old man came and peered in the window. As he watched the pages flicking out of the machine, he clapped his hand over his mouth in astonishment. "I've always heard they can write books fast, but I didn't believe it," he exclaimed. "Now I've seen it with my own eyes!"

"This is the Bible I'm printing. Do you know what that is?" I asked. He didn't. So very simply I recounted the story of God's creation of man. His traditional religion had already taught him that. Then I told him of man's sin and of God's love so great that he sent his only Son to earth to die in order to take our punishment so that we could be forgiven. I told him that God's son who died came back to life and now wants us to accept him so that we can live with him forever.

The old man had never heard the story before. He listened with wonder. When I paused, he rushed back to the path, grabbed a few people, saying, "Come hear the most wonderful news anybody every heard!" Pulling them to the window, he pointed at me and commanded, "Tell it again."

Again and again he went and called others to the window. The crowd was so packed around the window I could scarcely breathe. I continued changing stencils, turning the mimeograph, perspiring, and telling over and over the wonderful message of God's love. When it got late, I recalled that I had some Gospels of John in their language so I distributed them to the crowd. In a few days the government moved all the refugees to a distant location. I never saw them again but I remembered that God said, "My word shall not return unto me void . . . . " Somehow I hope I'll see that old man in heaven as well as others who heard of God's love that day.

Periodically as I typed, when sufficient material was

The first Kirundi Bibles came to Kibuye, Burundi, in 1968. Joseph, on right, was my translation assistant for 13 years.

ready, the committee of 20 met to read through the translation. Since the translator was on furlough in England, I was
asked to work with the committee. One man walked 100 miles
to be there. Another rode a bicycle 40 miles. Others rode on
trucks or were brought by missionaries.

Divided into two groups which worked simultaneously,
they read aloud from 7:00 a.m. until 12:00, and from 2:00 until
6:00, then met all together in the evenings to discuss any
problems encountered and make final decisions. All the Bible
was examined in this way. Then it was my task to prepare a
perfect copy to send to the Bible Society in London for printing.

About 10 years earlier when the New Testament in
Kirundi first arrived in the country, one man came to buy his
Bible for which he had been saving money for some time.
When the book was placed in his hands, he went away hug-
ging it, exclaiming over and over, "I've got God's Word! I've got
God's Word!"

Realizing the transforming power of the Word of God
often eased the tedium of long hours of typing. How precious
the Bible is! There were times when the words I was typing
came to me like a flash of light, lifting my spirits and giving
me new strength.

The task was not finished with the sending of the manuscript to the Bible Society. Several years later, when finally the
printing was in progress, the proofs were sent back to
Burundi to be read. Usually at least three people read them
aloud together: Rosemary the translator, a Murundi literature
worker, and myself. A complete reading like that took us
about three months. The proofs were read and corrected three
times, each time going back to London for the corrections to
be made.

On the third and final reading we found a heading that

was supposed to say, "It is grace alone that saves us (*buduk-iza*)." But the second "u" had been made an "a" *(budakiza)*, which made it say, "It is grace alone that does not save." So even the mundane task of proof-reading was of great importance.

All this was made worthwhile when we saw the Word at work in people's lives. Once Joseph, my assistant translator, was preaching. Holding up his Bible, he said, "This Book works. I know it works! Yesterday a neighbor's child died suddenly and they sent for me. I took my Bible and read to them some words from Job. Later in the evening the grieving mother came to my house and said, 'Do you have that Book? Bring that Book and your songs and come to our house.' So I took them and went. I read from the Word and sang to them about heaven. Then we prayed and Jesus came down and wiped away their tears. It was a miracle! I was amazed to see what the Word did to them. Then they begged me to leave the Word with them. This Book works!"

Yes, thank God, it works, and what transformations it has brought about in the lives of many! A year later this family had joined the church and was serving the Lord.

The Kirundi Bible finally came off the press in 1967. A beautiful service of dedication was held in which both Protestants and Catholics participated. Throughout the country in various churches services of praise for it were held with much rejoicing.

11. Promise Fulfilled

Life is made up of joy and sorrow, progress and delay, victories and losses. The presence of Jesus enables us to go through each of these experiences with courage and steadfastness.

During the months I was working on the Bible I began to have bouts of debilitating illness. It was finally diagnosed as typhoid fever (again!) and appropriate treatment was given. I would be very ill for a couple weeks, then feel fine for a time, then I would be down again. Repeated blood tests always came back strongly positive in spite of three courses of treatment.

July 1, 1962, was the long-awaited Independence Day. For the Barundi it was a day of great rejoicing and celebrating. For the foreigners there was much apprehension in view of what had happened in the Congo. But our fears were never realized. No great upheaval took place, and though there were occasional shouts of "White man, go home," we sensed little antagonism beyond what we had seen for some months.

Evelyn Rupert (Heath), Ila Gunsolus (Jacobs), and I were

booked to leave two days later for a month's vacation in Nairobi. The day before Independence my purse was stolen from the car as I sat right beside it. It contained my check books, some cash, my passport, driver's license, air ticket to Nairobi and other items.

What a dilemma! All businesses were closed for the holiday and the next day offices would be manned by new African personnel. Yet in the Lord's great goodness, by the evening of July 2, all my documents were replaced including passport and permanent residence card! The following day we arrived in Nairobi.

I was told to see a doctor there for further medical evaluation as my first order of business. The doctor promptly put me in the hospital for contagious diseases. After considerable

Spring Arbor College began the Alumnus of the Year program in 1963, and I was the first recipient! Though I felt far from deserving such an honor, I was pleased to see the College expressing its world-wide concern in selecting a missionary for this recognition.

treatment and blood tests that were still positive, the doctor said I must return to the States. A few hours after I received that word, a cable came saying my mother had died of a heart attack. Had it been my father I would not have been surprised. He had recently had two serious strokes and was barely able to walk. Now, ill as I was, my father really needed me. So I returned to Burundi, put my affairs in order, packed up my belongings, and was soon back in Elsie, Michigan, with my father. I had served only five years of what should have been a six-year term.

Toward the end of the year after further treatment I finally got a negative result on my blood test and was pronounced cured of typhoid. Feeling unable to care for my father's house and property, I moved Dad to an apartment in Spring Arbor near my brother Keith and his family.

It was wonderful to be among many old friends in Spring Arbor, and meet new ones. Days were filled with caring for Dad, doing some translation, and especially working on a concordance of the Kirundi New Testament. I also did a quarter's work at Michigan State University in order to keep my teaching certificate valid, and of course there was frequent weekend ministry in various churches near and rather far.

What a surprise it was when at Commencement in 1963 I was honored as Spring Arbor College's first Alumnus of the Year! Though I felt far from deserving such an honor, I was pleased that the College expressed its world-wide concern in selecting a missionary for this recognition.

Frequent letters from Africa urged me to return in the summer, for a teacher was badly needed. But another stroke put my Dad back in the hospital for a month. There was no way I could leave him unless some other provision was found for his care.

As I prayed for the Lord's guidance and for his will to be done, I felt I had the assurance that I would be returning to Burundi. I interpreted that to mean at the end of a normal one-year furlough. Later, one day as I was driving along, it seemed that the Lord impressed on me very strongly the words, "I believe God that it shall be even as it was told me." I felt again that surely this was confirmation that I would return that summer. Throughout all that time I never told my dad of the letters that came pleading for my speedy return to Burundi. In my love for him, I did not want him to be troubled by this pull in two directions.

But fall came, and no provision had been found for my father's care. I accepted a part-time position teaching French and English Composition at Spring Arbor College. This was challenging and enjoyable. Yet my heart was troubled.

Somehow I had misinterpreted the Lord's guidance. One day as I was praying, I said, "Lord, I guess I don't know how to understand your guidance, for I thought you gave me that

My dad in his room at Gerry Homes. He seldom missed a week of writing to me, though he could no longer hold a pen in his fingers. He pecked out the words on a little old typewriter we got for him.

verse." The next day in my daily Bible reading I came to that very verse the Lord had given me (Acts 27:25), and was astonished to discover it was followed by: "Howbeit we must first be cast up on a certain island." God said to me, "This is your island." How tenderly and lovingly the Lord leads us! I went on from there with joy.

A few months later I read in Jeremiah 33:14: "Behold, the days come, saith the Lord, that I will perform that good thing that I have promised." So clearly came the message: "This is for you."

After a few days Dad said: "It isn't right for you to stay here to take care of me when you are so badly needed in Africa. I want you to try to get me into one of our Free Methodist retirement centers."

I privately made a list of nine things that needed to be accomplished if I were to return to Burundi that year. Four months later all had been taken care of.

When the director of Gerry Homes in New York State understood our situation, he made a place for Dad without the usual two to three years on the waiting list. Early in June my brother Bruce and I took Dad to Gerry, where he was given a lovely, cheerful room, and he settled in happily. In August, on my way back to Burundi, I stopped and spent a few days with Dad. He said, "I'm happier here than I could be anywhere else, other than in my own home." Dad had made up his mind to be happy.

During the years that followed he seldom missed a week of writing to me, though he could no longer hold a pen in his fingers. He pecked out the words on a little old typewriter we got for him. There was never a word of complaint but only accounts of how good everyone was to him.

Five years after taking Dad to Gerry Homes I was home on

another furlough and had the privilege of standing beside his bed as he went to be with the Lord (see ch. 16).

12. Give Me A Little Book

Arriving back in Burundi, I was assigned this time to our Alliance teacher training school at Kibimba where I served in 1952-1956. It was a joy to again train youth for the future. But to my consternation, when the school director, an English missionary, prepared the teaching schedule, I was to teach music, art, physics and chemistry. My problem was that I can't carry a tune, I can't draw a picture, and I had never studied physics or chemistry!

I also had some French and English classes for which I felt better qualified. The students learned a lot of music *theory* that year, the missionary doctor enjoyed doing some experiments for the science classes, and I learned that the Lord can see you through seemingly impossible situations.

Along with their secular lessons, the students were learning and growing in their walk with Christ. In writing an essay for French class one young man wrote: "How you can recognize a Christian: If you're a Christian your whole family knows it, and so do the animals in the kraal (the enclosed house and yard). The man whose garden is next to yours knows it, too. When a man is a Christian he gives his wife the key to the money box and he isn't always asking her where she hoed that day. When a woman is a Christian she isn't always begging her husband for new clothes."

One day another missionary, Kathryn Hendrix (Vance), and I drove to Bujumbura. Just before we reached the city, the car stalled. Kathryn went for help while I stayed to watch the car. Seeing the throngs of people passing by, I remembered we had some Kirundi tracts in the glove compartment, so I began handing them out. In moments the car was surrounded by people with outstretched hands begging for a tract.

One little boy carrying a huge load of wood on his head, almost heavier than he could manage, saw the tracts in others' hands. Laboriously putting down his load, he came and asked for one. Then he just stood there and read it through. Finally, getting a passer-by to help him get his load on again, he turned and flashed me a radiant smile of thanks and went on.

A man coming by read his tract, then turned and went back in the direction he had just come from. Soon the supply of tracts was exhausted, but still the people came to plead for a little book, some even with tears. Long afterward, people who met others far down the road with a tract in their hands came running to the car to ask for one. One woman almost wept as she begged me to try to find one more. My heart wept, too, as I saw this desperate hunger for the Word.

On another occasion when I was in Bujumbura, sitting in the car waiting for someone, a crippled beggar came to beg from me so I gave him a tract. He sat down right there and read it through. Others saw him and came to ask for a tract. Whether well-dressed or poor, nearly everyone passing by wanted "a little book."

One man began to ask me questions which gave me the opportunity to explain the way of salvation. Soon a little crowd had gathered round and the questioner was deeply moved by what he heard. When I left in a few minutes, I went on my way praying that the seed would bear fruit.

During the summer vacation three of us single missionaries drove to Mwanza in western Tanzania for some rest and renewal. At one place the car had to go on a ferry to cross an arm of Lake Victoria. Besides several vehicles there were many pedestrians on the ferry. Part way across a completely unoffical-looking African in ordinary clothes came around carrying a syringe. To our amazement, he was giving compulsory smallpox vaccinations to everybody with no sterilization of needle or arms! We managed to escape by hastily producing our vaccination certificates.

While in Mwanza we decided to make a visit to the Serengeti, a vast game reserve about a three-hour drive from Mwanza. Roads there are not paved and in the dry season, which this was, they were pure dust! As soon as we entered the reserve we began to see herds of thousands of wildebeest (or gnu). I think I had never guessed there were as many animals in the world as we saw there, gradually migrating to wherever they could find pasture. They were accompanied by huge herds of zebra. What a spectacle!

That day we also saw hundreds of graceful gazelles and impala (both of the deer family), and many giraffe, buffalo, hyenas, ostriches, vultures, baboons, some prides of lion, and even a leopard. Beautiful birds of various colors flitted among the trees and bushes.

The variety and magnitude of God's creation boggles the mind and makes one feel like bowing in awe before him. As we returned to our place of lodging we were tired and dusty, but filled with gratitude to God for the privilege of observing nature relatively untouched by man.

13. Political Tensions

In the countries of Rwanda and Burundi live three ethnic groups: the Tutsi, Hutu and Twa (*Batutsi*, *Bahutu*, and *Batwa* in their languages). The Twa, about 1% of the population, are a pygmoid people generally despised by the rest of the population. They were the earliest inhabitants of the area. Traditionally, they have been nomadic, moving from place to place, and earning their living by hunting or by making clay pots used for cooking.

While I was working with the Laubach team at Kibimba (see chapter 6), a group of us visited a nearby pygmy settlement. I was designated to give a little talk to the 40 or 50 people who gathered while we sang some hymns in their language. As simply as I knew how I told of man's sin and God's redemption through Jesus, provided just because of his great love for us all.

After I finished, a little old man grabbed my arm and said, "This is the most wonderful news we've ever heard -- but I'm too old to learn something new. But see, here are our little boys. Won't you take them and teach them?" In time some of those children did go to the mission school.

The Hutu make up about 84% of the population, are of the tribes and languages known as Bantu, and are cultivators. Probably they came into the region from the north and west, maybe as early as the second or third century A.D. Much later, about the 15th century, the Tutsi with their long-horned cattle migrated to this area, most likely originating in Ethiopia.

Though they were only a small minority of the population (presently about 15%), the Tutsi gradually dominated the other peoples. They retained power until about 1959 in Rwanda, and until 1993 in Burundi.

Belgium governed these two countries as a trusteeship under the United Nations (originally the League of Nations) from soon after World War I until their independence in 1962. French has been the official language. The African language of Burundi is Kirundi, spoken by all three groups. The African language of Rwanda is Kinyarwanda. Both Kirundi and Kinyarwanda are Bantu-based languages, the original language of the Hutu. The two are very similar. Considerable intermarriage has taken place between the Tutsi and the Hutu.

The relations of these two larger groups have been a source of conflict on many occasions. As we entered the school year in the fall of 1965, we were about to undergo some of these effects. A change of directors occurred at the school when the English missionary left for furlough and Randall Brown of the Friends replaced him.

In October an uprising occurred in Bujumbura, the capital. The king fled to another country, the prime minister was shot, and a number of people killed. Two days later we could see smoke in the distance in various directions where homes were being burned. Trees were felled across the roads to prevent cars from travelling. Our U. S. ambassador told us to have a suitcase packed and a plan of departure ready in case we should have to leave suddenly. The conflict spread across the country and many lives were lost including some of our Christian people.

Needless to say, these events produced much fear and unrest among our students who belonged to both tribal groups. They began to mistrust each other. Finally about half of them fled. Randall kept in touch with the government offices and was told the students must come back and school go on.

Finally, one morning about 7:00 a truck load of soldiers drove in to the mission station. Some came to guard my house, some to Randall's, some to the house where our radio transmitter was located. Others went to the school, about a half mile away, to question the students individually. Soon two officials and two soldiers came to search my house, while another with a gun stood just outside the big picture window, keeping me in his sights. I never knew what they were looking for. It was with great relief I saw them leave, though they left everything in the house turned upside down.

In the meantime they told Randall Brown that he, with his wife and two children, must prepare to leave in one hour. They were not allowed to speak to any of us, not even to turn over school business and finances to anyone, nor could we approach their house. An hour later the Browns and a soldier got in their car and a jeep-load of soldiers followed them as they made their way to Bujumbura. With the help of the U. S. Embassy, they left for the U. S. a few days later, less than three months after they arrived in Burundi.

Orders were left for us to carry on school as usual! Imagine the chaos! Some students were still away, others were

The gardeners read our monthly Christian magazine
Burakeye, which means "Day has dawned."

full of fear, trusting no one, and our staff was reduced. The responsibility for directing the school fell on me, along with teaching 36 hours a week. Without God's help this would have been an impossibility. But in the midst of all these pressures, God gave me his peace and strength. He never fails us!

About three weeks later I had to have some minor surgery. While I was under the anesthetic, a messenger came from the government to say they were going to do with me as they had with Randall. Not being able to talk with me then, the message was never officially delivered to me, though I learned of it. Reports soon came, again unofficially, that our school was going to be closed and I would be sent out of the country.

Finally, the head of the national Education Office arrived and told me to call all the students together. I thought, "This is it!" Addressing them he said, "I want you to forget about politics and get busy and study. Your school is not going to be closed and none of your professors will be sent away. Now get serious about your studies!" I was dumbfounded and could scarcely believe my ears. It was he who only a few days before had said he would close the school. God had performed a miracle!

After sending the students back to their classes, the official assured me of his full support and cooperation. He said he would report that very day to the provincial authorities that all was calm at school, and they should harass us no more.

We learned later that a disgruntled former teacher fed the local government officials many lies about the school, which had brought on much of the trouble. Now things settled down, both in the school and in the country, and I continued my work of directing the school, teaching, serving as treasurer of the Free Methodist Mission, and occasionally squeezing in some time for literature projects.

Early in 1966 it became necessary for me to go to Kampala, Uganda, for major surgery. Olive Bodtcher (Downs) accompanied me and Evelyn Rupert (Heath) carried out my responsibilities at Kibimba during my two-month absence.

Increasingly, the need for Christian books was being felt throughout the country, and the longing to help meet this need burned in my heart and also in the minds of others, both missionaries and Africans. Before the end of the school year the Alliance of Protestant Missions wrote our Mission Board requesting that I be released from teaching to give full time to the production of literature. Our Board agreed, so as we were winding up the school year, I packed up all my belongings to move back to Kibuye where I had begun my service in Burundi.

During that year one of our students was Abeli, whose parents were Christians. His father was a Bible translator in Congo. Abeli wrote in a French essay, "I'm only a head Christian, not a heart Christian." How many others, both in Africa and in America, would say the same thing if they were truthful! After that I talked with him several times about his need. He expressed a desire to join in his father's work of translating and assented to all I said, but when I asked him what kept him from accepting Christ, he would say, "I really don't know." Many prayers were offered for him.

At last, graduation day came with no apparent change in Abeli's position. His parents came from Congo for the occasion. When Abeli received his diploma, he walked over and handed it to his father, indicating, "You are the one who made this possible."

After the ceremonies Abeli came to my house to tell me goodbye. As I was congratulating him on his success, he said, "But, Mademoiselle, there's still one thing lacking."

"What is that?" I asked though I was sure I knew.

"I still don't have Jesus in my heart," he replied.

I asked, "Would you like us to pray about it now?"

He would. We sat down in the midst of my packing boxes ready to be moved and shared some Scripture verses. Then Abeli prayed: "Lord, I know I'm a sinner. I'm filthy and I'm empty. My morality can't save me, and my parents' religion can't save me. I believe you're going to save me some day. Amen."

Looking up at him, I said, "Why did you say 'some day'?

What are you waiting for? Jesus wants to save you now. He's just waiting for you."

Quickly he bowed his head again and prayed, "Lord Jesus, forgive my sins, come into my heart, take charge of my life right now." Joy and assurance were written on his face when he looked up again. Now he was ready to go out and meet the challenges that life offered him.

14. Too Late

I happily settled in at Kibuye. Mine was the oldest house
on the station, built with sun-dried bricks and thus a favorite
abode of termites. The walls were thick and the windows
small, so little sunshine reached inside. The temperature in
the house rarely got up to 70 degrees, so I had a fire in my
fireplace nearly every evening, which I enjoyed immensely.
The altitude at Kibuye is 6,000 feet.

Soon after my return there, I met Emanuweli on the path.
He was the man whose story is told in Chapter Six who
learned to read by the Laubach method. Since then he had
drifted away from the Lord. Often over the years I had prayed
for him, but there seemed to be no response. Now, meeting
him face to face for the first time in years, I talked to him
about his spiritual need and said I'd been praying for him. He
admitted his need and thanked me heartily for speaking to
him about it. Nearly a month later he came to church. When
the invitation was given to pray at the altar, he went forward.

He prayed with great sobs and wept a little pool of tears.

His testimony showed deep and complete repentance. He said one of his greatest griefs was that he had kept his wife and children from coming to church. As soon as the service was over he wanted to buy a Bible. I loaned him one until another day. He testified it was the words I spoke to him on the path that started him wanting to return to the Lord.

I found joy in renewing acquaintance with many Barundi whom I had known before. I was always thrilled to have news of my former students now serving in various parts of the country.

Binyoni was a very serious student, conscientious about his work, committed to the Lord, and gifted with a beautiful tenor voice. After he graduated, he became principal of the elementary school on a Friends (Quaker) mission station. Here is his account of an experience he had:

"My sister was sick. She was taken to many doctors but they were unable to help her. She would fall on the floor, day or night, and sometimes the illness would attack her in the night and she would wander off on the hills to sleep.

"I began to think: I believe she is demon possessed. God has promised in his Word that those who believe in him will be able to cast out demons. I feel as if I have faith for that. Here's this poor girl sick day and night! How worn out my mother is in caring for her. I shall get someone with a car to go with me and bring her to my house. I'll call the Christians together and we'll pray for her. I believe that God will cast out that demon from her.

"I immediately got up and went and got the girl, though some doubted it would do any good. I told my mother and others, 'She will come back a well girl.'

"When we got to my house I called others to come and gather round my sister to pray for her. We knelt and prayed, ignoring how ill she was, and how on the way coming she tried to break the car windows, shouting, 'Let *us* go, you're taking *us* to a bad place.' We prayed, 'Lord Jesus, we believe your promises. Cast out the demon from this girl. We believe you are here and Satan cannot stay.' A great faith filled us as we continued to pray on through the night. She still seemed no better.

"In the morning I had to go about two miles away on my bike for some school business. As I rode home, I heard the voice of God tell me, 'Your sister is healed.' Immediately I got off my bike, stood with bowed head, and thanked God for the wonderful miracle he had performed. When I reached home, my sister met me saying, 'Praise the Lord! Just a few minutes ago I was delivered, and I'm well!' How we rejoiced together! Jesus has all power."

* * * * * * * *

Sibomana, a former student, was a patient in the T. B. sanitarium for several years. Once when I visited him, he gave a beautiful testimony of his salvation and said that sometimes he longed for the angels to come and take him to be with Jesus. I tried to write to him from time to time to keep him encouraged, and occasionally sent him some things he needed.

One day a letter came from him saying that they needed milk and protein foods rarely available at the sanitarium. I had abundant supplies of these things which good friends in America had sent. I determined to send some to him at once. Then I got busy.

Sometimes after I went to bed at night I'd think about Sibomana and tell myself, "Tomorrow I must get a package ready to send to him." The next day brought its busy round of responsibilities, and once again it slipped my mind. I did care about this lad. His letters were full of courage and trust and praise. He had no family that paid any attention to him. He first became ill just before Christmas while a student at Kibimba. I tried to cheer his otherwise bleak holiday with some little gifts and goodies and decorations for his hospital room. Thus he became my fast friend. During these years I prayed for him, visited him, wrote to him. It seemed he had no one else to care. But I was busy! From time to time as he came to my mind I prayed for him and promised myself I would do something at once. But the days slipped by.

At last one day I felt I must put it off no longer so I got the package ready, sent it to a pastor who lived near the sanatorium, and asked him to deliver it. Just a few days later my package came back with the word that Sibomana died two days before my package was taken to him! Too late! Why had I delayed so long?

I do not deceive myself that the things I sent could have saved his life. The disease had gone too far for that. But they could have comforted his lonely heart. They could have reminded him that the love of Jesus was manifest in another person. They could have spoken to him of God's compassion and care. But they were too late! So Sibomana lived out his last days and died alone, perhaps thinking that no one cared for his soul.

It is so easy to let the busyness of every day keep us from the ministry Christ would have us do for others.

* * * * * * * *

Now at Kibuye I could really give my time to literature work, yet it was easy to let the hours be dissipated on other

things: training a new cook, entertaining guests (they were
many because of the hospital on the station), looking after my
garden and training a gardener (we had no other source of
fresh vegetables), mission treasury business, and even teaching Kirundi to the other missionaries.

Other things interrupted the routine, too. A necessary
part of the household was having a cat, the only alternative to
rats and mice. Having lost my cat, I was offered a cute little
part-Siamese kitten by a missionary in Bujumbura. But the
poor thing cried all the time and wouldn't eat. Looking it over,
I found in a paw what I thought was a jigger (or, chigger).
These are little pests that burrow in under the skin, especially
around a toenail, and develop a sack of eggs there. They are
best removed with a safety pin, laying back the skin to expose
the sack and lifting it out without breaking it. Africans are
more adept at doing this than Westerners, probably because
they have more experience at it.

When I tried to remove the jigger while a friend held the
kitten still, instead of a jigger, out popped a little white larva,
about the size of the end of my little finger. Examining further, we eventually removed 36 of those! I learned later that
the larva were from the mango fly, and this kitten began its
life under a mango tree. Once freed of those pests, it became a
beautiful and useful cat.

Many were the trials and humorous incidents in training
new workers. Once I had five guests who were sitting in the
living room. I told the cook to prepare for six of us, yet when I
came in the table was set for four.

"Didn't I tell you that we would be six?" I asked.

"Yes," he replied, "but you only have four chairs." He did-
n't realize I planned to borrow some chairs from my neighbor.

On another occasion my cook was a girl. She nicely prepared my supper, called me to come and eat, but forgot to set the table!

Another time my pancakes were a strange color. The cook used chili powder in place of baking powder. These words had to be written in English in the recipe because Kirundi has no word for them. She had seen the word 'powder' on the can!

One day I heard strange scraping sounds in the kitchen. On investigating I found my new cook using my best paring knife to scrape the teflon off a skillet. She thought it was dirt!

A friend sent me some seasoning packets, one of which was for Spanish rice. The cook had learned how to make Spanish rice from scratch but with guests there I decided we'd use the mix. I thought I'd explained to him sufficiently how to use it but when we came to the table, here was a dish of soupy, tomato stuff, without a grain of rice in it. I called the cook and asked, "Where's the rice?" He replied, "I know you can't see it, but it says 'Spanish rice' on the package, so it's there whether you can see it or not."

Equipment failures were frustrating, but sometimes good for a laugh. Our three hours an evening of electricity depend-ed on a temperamental diesel generator, so kerosene lamps were kept handy and ready for use. The government installed a water system that used a pump operated by a diesel motor which frequently failed. A capable African mechanic who worked for us could sometimes solve the problems. Once he described the water pump set-up like this: "This diesel has a big fuel tank. The tank has two stomachs, an upper and a lower. The string that goes from the stomach to the motor has a wound in it and is too flat on the ground."

On another occasion when the generator was giving us trouble I returned from a few days away and asked how the generator was doing. He replied, "Just fine! It hasn't had a cold or a stomach ache since you went away."

Mechanical equipment was not our only source of problems. We had to hire a watchman to protect our gardens and property from thieves. One of them *sold* to some young boys the privilege of stealing our avocados!

We found that pineapples were disappearing from my garden every Sunday during church. One day my houseboy said, "There's a youngster out here the pastor has sent to repent of stealing pineapples."

I went out and asked the lad what he had come to tell me. He blurted out, "They've lied about me and said I stole your pineapples."

I asked, "Is that what the pastor sent you to tell me?"

He replied, "No, but I didn't steal any pineapples; it was strawberries!" Finally he gave a little memorized speech asking forgiveness for stealing and saying he wouldn't do it any more.

I gave him a little talk on stealing. Then I said, "Now if you'd stay in church on Sundays you wouldn't be tempted to steal like this."

"Oh, no," he said, "it wasn't on Sunday I stole your pineapples -- whoops, I mean strawberries, it was on Wednesday!" I concluded the repentance wasn't very real.

15. Home Evangelism

Many people think if one is doing translation work he must be translating the Bible. But that was not my task. There were great needs for other materials: helps for pastors, Sunday school teaching guides, church membership instruction, devotional books, and many others. I began to prepare a concordance of the New Testament and a series of Sunday school books during my "spare" time while teaching. Now I set about to complete these projects, as well as to prepare a set of lessons for pastors and lay ministers to use in teaching church membership classes.

For this type of work it is essential to have the help of a national. We foreigners rarely master all the intricacies of the language. We never quite learn to "think black." The church leaders suggested I hire Joseph Twaha, a Bible school graduate, to work with me. What an excellent choice he proved to be! I heard Africans say of him, "He has a wider vocabulary range than anyone we know." However, he knew no French and only a little English.

Typing material translated in my home at Kibuye in 1969.

This meant that I had to do the initial translating and then check everything with him. Then I had to do the typing and in some cases mimeograph the materials. Some books were printed at the inter-mission press that was developed at Mweya, an hour's drive from Kibuye. Other books were printed at larger presses in other countries. After several years of working this way, Noah Nzeyimana, freshly graduated from Seminary, joined our staff. He was fluent in French and English and could type reasonably well. He was a real answer to prayer.

In 1985 Noah was elected the first African Bishop of the Provisional General Conference of the Free Methodist Church in Burundi. He still continues in that office.

Soon after Joseph began working with me we set up a little bookstore and reading room, the first of its kind at any of our stations. The small reading area became very popular with the elementary school children during their noon hour.

So many came that Joseph had to limit both the number who came in at a time and the time they could stay. This arrangement gave everyone a turn. Their favorite book? *Sears Catalog!* Remember that even yet the number of books existing in their language was very small.

One day an illiterate woman came in to buy a Bible. Joseph asked her, "What do you plan to do with your Bible?"

"Oh," she exclaimed with a smile, "I'll keep it in my home. Every time I have a visitor I'll ask him if he can read. If he can, I'll ask him to read to me from my Bible. That way I'll get to hear it and so will he!" Home evangelism!

A patient at the hospital, who was not yet a Christian, wandered into the bookstore one day and decided to buy a hymn book. A couple days later he returned and said to Joseph, "This book won't do me much good unless I can sing the songs. Won't you teach me some of them?" So they sang together for an hour. Then he asked Joseph what the words meant.

Joseph explained that we are all sinners. Jesus died for us so that we can be forgiven if we accept him. They prayed together and the man found the peace of sins forgiven. A bit later he said, "I've had more joy in these few minutes than I ever got from all the beer I've drunk all my life!" Then he said he wanted to buy a Bible as soon as he got the money.

Joseph came to me laughing with joy as he told this, thrilled that he had helped someone find Christ. After some weeks Joseph confirmed that this man's life gave evidence of the transformation Christ had brought about.

Various difficulties came, too. We received a lovely Gestetner mimeograph machine, only slightly used, from the Spring Arbor Church, but somehow it got out of adjustment. I fiddled and fiddled with it but could not make it feed right, so I wrote to the company, described the trouble, and asked for instructions. They sent me a portion of their manual used by their repair men. It was terribly complicated, and when I took the outside case off the machine, it was more so. There must have been a million parts!

At last I sat down in desperation beside the machine and prayed, "Now, Lord, you know how badly I need this machine. Please heal it or give me the brains to figure out what this book says." Then, following the instructions and diagrams, I did step by step what it said, even though I didn't understand how or what I was doing, even making adjustments of 1/32 of an inch. When I put it back together it worked beautifully!

Later, while I was on furlough, someone else borrowed the machine. The trip produced the same maladjustment it had had before. When I got back, I thought I knew what to do, so I "fixed" it, but it didn't work. Once again I had to acknowledge my need and seek the Lord's help. After that, when I went through the procedure and put it back together again, once more it worked just fine. How willing the Lord is to help us in our need, but we have to acknowledge that "without him we can do nothing."

Someone was knocking at the door. Leaving my work in my office, I went to answer. The front door of my living room was half glass, and as I looked out, no one was there. I stepped up closer to look better. No one! But still I heard the knocking sound. I tried to open the door, but it stuck. Looking down at the floor, I was startled to see the head of a puff adder (a deadly snake) just three inches from my toe. And I had on tennis shoes.

I did what most women would do under such circumstances. I yelled! The gardener came running, hoe in hand, and soon dispatched the snake. The sound I had heard was the screen door rattling as the snake tried to crawl under it. I trembled to think what might have happened had I just set my foot a few inches farther over. God protects, even when we don't have time to cry for help!

Let me add here my other snake story. Actually, over the years I saw very few snakes, though once I saw a python 21 feet long and five inches in diameter. One night after the lights were out (we had electricity for only three hours each evening from our diesel generator) I went to my kitchen carrying my flashlight. My cat jumped at something by my feet. Shining my light there, my heart almost stopped. I saw a black snake coiled between my feet as I took a step. Why it hadn't struck, other than God's restraint on it, I don't know.

This time a yell brought the night watchman. He took one look at the snake and said, "Oh, Mademoiselle, that snake's poison is so strong! If I hit it with this stick, its poison will go right up the stick into my arm!" Some snake! Nevertheless, he hit it, then quickly dropped his stick, leaving me to carry snake and stick outside.

In reality, I hated spiders worse than snakes (and there were more of them). Once as I sat by my table writing letters, I saw a spider as big as my hand (a tarantula?) between me and an overstuffed chair. I feared that if I moved he'd go up into the chair. Cautiously I sneaked away and grabbed a fly swatter. Praying, "Lord, help me get him on the first blow," I brought the swatter down *hard*. Success!

The Lord's protection surrounds us even when we are not aware of it. I'm confident that people's prayers for the missionaries have a great part in this. A woman wrote me, "Last week I was awakened in the night three different nights to pray for you. At first I didn't even know who you were but just woke up with the name Betty Ellen Cox on my mind. I had to look up in the *Missionary Tidings* to find something about you. What was your special need that I was called on to pray like that?"

I could think of nothing special happening at the time she indicated so I replied, "I do not know of any special danger or need I was in at that time. But that does not mean your call to pray was not real. It just means that God so protected me from whatever the danger was that I did not even know about it."

* * * * * * * * *

Visiting an outstation one Sunday, we found the little mud and grass church packed with people. An outstation is a location out on the hills where there is a church and a school of at least two or three grades, usually led by a lay minister.

On this occasion, opportunity for testimonies was given. A little old lady stood up. Her teeth were gone, her cheeks sunken, her hands calloused from a lifetime of swinging a hoe. Obviously, she had never known anything but having babies and cultivating the fields. But with beaming face she said, "I'm just an old lady and I don't know very much. But I know Jesus loves me and he lives at our house."

I marveled that the Holy Spirit was able to penetrate her untrained mind sufficiently with the truth of the gospel, that she knew the joy of sins forgiven and a real relationship with Jesus. Indeed, only by the work of the Holy Spirit do any of our efforts produce fruit that lasts. As Paul said in 1 Corinthians 3:6, "I have planted the seed, Apollos watered it, but God made it grow."

In general I was not regularly involved in the women's work of sewing classes and Bible studies. However, at times I was invited to be the speaker at their district or conference retreats when women came from all directions for two or three days of fellowship. On one occasion the retreat was to be at Mweya and I was to speak six or eight times. For days I had been trying to prepare but could get no inspiration.

Finally, I dropped on my knees and prayed, "Lord, I've got to have help. I can't do it."

His voice came saying, "Go on with your other work, I've taken over." Indeed he had! He led me to use the "Heart of Man" charts, a series of big posters showing the sinful heart filled with various animals representing different sins such as a lion for anger, a snake for deceit, and so on.

When forgiveness comes, all the animals have to leave and Christ enters bringing all the fruits of the Christian life. This was something the women could see and understand. From the first service they began to respond to these truths. In one service there were 29 seekers -- Catholics, pagans, backsliders. One, the wife of a cook in a missionary home, had long been the subject of many prayers.

Another woman testified: "We used to have such good times singing and praying together at our house. Then my husband started to drink, and I did, too, and Jesus went out of our home and didn't live there anymore. Lately I've gotten so lonesome to have Jesus come and live with us again. He came back to my heart today and I'm going to take him home with me."

Throughout the retreat women kept coming to Jesus. Long afterward they continued talking about those meetings. This was not anything that I had done, rather the Holy Spirit had taken over as he promised and allowed me to be his instrument.

Frequently women came to my home to seek counselling or encouragement, or just for friendship's sake. One young woman who came had an adulterous relationship with a young man from the Congo, thus a different tribe and different customs. They married and he took her to live in Bujumbura. Both had apparently repented and said they were living for the Lord. Yet, soon after their baby was born, he brought a second wife of his own tribe into the home and expected them to live together peacefully.

It was obvious that the second wife was favored, and he became mean and drank heavily. The young woman came home to our area and wanted my advice. Should she leave him or stay and endure a miserable life? She said, "I knew if I could just get to you, you have love and you get your wisdom from God, so I was sure you'd help me."

How should I advise her? We wept and prayed together. We recognized that sin, even when repented of, has consequences. Their marriage vows were made before God, so I encouraged her to go back and do her best to live a godly and loving life in that difficult situation. She did so, but only a few months later her husband put her out of the home, yet he kept the baby. She returned home to her parents sad and brokenhearted, but determined to serve the Lord.

* * * * * * * *

Political problems and tensions seemed almost endemic in the culture. Burundi always had a king of the Tutsi ethnic group to whom the people as a whole felt loyal. So the one in power at the time when independence was granted had continued in that position. In 1966, his son proclaimed himself king. However, three months later the head of the army seized power and proclaimed the country a republic instead of a kingdom. He proclaimed himself the prime minister.

From that time to the present there have been periodic eruptions of conflict between the two ethnic groups. Each time there is conflict many homes are burned, thousands of people are killed, and thousands more flee to neighboring countries.

We missionaries always avoided political involvement and refused to take sides. In our churches Tutsi and Hutu people worshipped together and no distinctions were made in the selection of church leaders. Usually, in times of conflicts, we felt quite safe, for violence was not directed at foreigners, although one time the U. S. Cultural Center in Bujumbura was attacked and sacked. Yet, on the advice of our Embassy, for long stretches of time we kept a suitcase packed with essentials, in case we should have to evacuate suddenly. Travel was often difficult at those times because barriers manned by soldiers were erected in many places to control the movement of people.

Sometimes we encountered as many as 10 barriers on the 100 mile trip from Kibuye to Bujumbura. At each stop it was necessary to show our documents including a permit to travel. Also, at times we were ordered to attend political rallies. We cooperated, though the speeches might include harangues against the white people.

In spite of these conflicts and tensions, the church was growing. We were thrilled when reports came in from the outlying churches of revivals where people were coming to Christ, 34 saved one week, 104 another, and many of these were first-time converts, coming out of their pagan religion and culture. The young man just starting to work for me was saved and continued faithful until his recent death.

We had a day watchman for the mission station and I had a gardener who worked for me. I began to notice they were missing at times when they should be working. I began to make inquiries but they always had a good explanation. One afternoon, again not finding them at work, I walked toward a little tavern near the mission property. There stood Yakobo, the watchman, quite obviously just finishing a drink. Kasa, the gardener, saw me, dropped to the ground, and began to roll over and over to get behind a little knoll. I called out and advised him to save his energy as I'd already seen him. Then I went home.

Later they came to me and appeared to be ashamed but denying that they'd been drinking. When I asked Yakobo what it was that I smelled, he said, "Oh! I stink, do I?"

They were very argumentative so I sent them home. They began to tell everyone, "Miss Cox says that all Barundi stink." After church leaders dealt with them, they were allowed to continue working with the warning that another offense would cost them their jobs. That is what happened a bit later.

A couple of months after this, shortly before Christmas, Yakobo came to my door and humbly and brokenly asked my forgiveness for the bad feelings he held toward me and the lies he had told. He said, "I've been so miserable over my sins that I couldn't sleep nights. I felt I couldn't face Christmas in this awful darkness. I couldn't forget the things you've taught us, the burden you've carried for us, and the people who have been saved through your ministry." We prayed together for forgiveness for him and soon the darkness vanished. His face was alight with joy.

Problems with workers were many , as the people were moving from a pagan culture to Christian principles. Many, many hours were spent in small local committees trying to solve a theft at the hospital or in a missionary's home, or dealing with a trusted employee who was found drunk. Usually one or more pastors would be in the committee, for they understand their own people better than we foreigners do.

The question of alcoholic drinks was a difficult one, for beer is such an important part of their culture. Until Christian teaching began to take effect, no business transactions were ever done without sharing drinks. Drinking was the most common cause of failure in new Christians. The coming of Coca-Cola and its easy availability provided a solution for many.

Once a group of teachers sent a petition to annual conference asking that the rules of the church be bent so it would be all right to drink "a little bit of beer." Some soundly converted, steadfast pastors took a strong stand against such compromise, even at the cost of losing some friends. Once in Rwanda this issue was so serious that the church almost split over it. Pastor Aaron (later to become bishop) and some others stood firm. The conference held to the Free Methodist position against alcoholic beverages. More than 200 members left the church in favor of their alcohol, but in the two years that followed, God sent a revival and far more new members were gained than were lost.

* * * * * * * *

Much of my time was taken up in inter-mission, or interchurch activities. Denominational lines are more blurred on the mission field as we collaborate on many projects aimed at evangelizing the country. World Gospel Mission, the Friends (evangelical Quakers), Free Methodists and other holiness groups united in a Bible school, a printing press, a school for missionary children at Mweya, and a bookstore and literature center in Gitega.

The Alliance of Protestant Missions (later, Churches)

worked together in a Literature Fellowship, Radio Cordac, Education Committee, language examinations for missionaries, and various other activities. I was called upon to serve on many of these committees which required frequent trips. The marvel is that I was able to do any literature work at all!

We missionaries tried to get in a two- or three-week vacation each year and nearly always came back refreshed and with a new perspective on our work. The various missions working in the country acquired a peninsula named Kumbya on Lake Kivu in Rwanda. It was about five miles from our Kibogora mission station. Here the different organizations had built cottages for simple lodging facilities and united in constructing a large building containing a dining room, kitchen, and a room for worship.

Each year in July or August an eight-day missionaries' retreat was held here for all denominations. The retreat was attended by 150 to 200 people including children. Many of them lived in tents or grass huts constructed for the occasion. Noted speakers came from overseas such as J. Edwin Orr, Corrie ten Boom, Oswald Smith, and many others.

All year long the missionaries looked forward with eagerness to this time of fellowship, swimming, renewal, and deepening our Christian walk. Quite a number of missionary children were saved in the children's or youth meetings at Kumbya. Sadly, in the violence of 1994 all the buildings there were looted and destroyed.

One year following the Kumbya retreat, Stan and Eileen Lehman with their three young children, Evelyn Rupert (Heath) and I drove in a Land Rover to Nairobi, Kenya, a distance of about 1,000 miles. Nairobi is a large city with a great mixture of the modern and the traditional. During the two weeks there most of my time was occupied with overseeing the printing of a Sunday school teachers' manual I translated into Kirundi, and reading proofs for it.

Returning to Burundi we travelled through Tanzania, visiting the Ngorongoro Crater park and the vast Serengeti game reserve. The scenes we saw were fabulous: Mt. Kilimanjaro with an altitude of 19,000 feet and Mt. Meru at 10,000 feet, the tropical rain forest around Ngorongoro, though brown, dry plains were elsewhere. The crater itself is nine miles across and 2,000 feet from rim to floor. Game of nearly all kinds can be seen on the floor of the crater including thousands of pink flamingos on a blue lake. Such an experience made us want to worship the Creator of it all. It was exciting to see prides of lions, groups of giraffes, herds of elephants, and more, all in their natural habitat. Then the trip through the Serengeti teeming with animals was beyond imagination.

Before reaching Ngorongoro we were reminded of God's loving care of us. The sound of a flapping tire caused us to stop. Stan jacked up the vehicle, then crawled under to check on something. Just moments after he emerged from under the vehicle the jack broke and the car slammed down. Stan would have been crushed had he remained under there just a moment longer.

About two minutes later a police car stopped with three men in it. One was a mechanic who had the necessary equipment to lift the car off the road. In a few minutes the tire was changed and we were on our way rejoicing and praising God. The rest of the vacation was uneventful and relaxing. When we reached home safely we felt renewed and ready to tackle our work again.

16. Why Furloughs?

Furlough time again, my fourth one! Returning to the U. S. this time included two very interesting experiences. In Nairobi, Kenya, it was my privilege and delight to attend a meeting to promote literacy and literature throughout Africa. About 30 people attended, some government officials, some Muslims, many missionaries, but all keenly concerned about developing literacy programs. The leader and organizer was a committed Christian with a concern to make literacy a means of reaching people for Christ. She did not hesitate to give clear witness to this even though some participants were not interested in Christianity.

During the 12-day conference a constitution was drawn up and the organization was founded and named Afrolit. All the participants became charter members. The conference included lectures, panels, committees, and much sharing of ideas and experiences. In the years that followed I was usually able to participate in the biennial meetings that occurred in various countries of Africa.

For example, in 1970 the meeting took place in Kinshasa, Zaire. Myra Adamson and I flew there right after the Kumbya retreat. En route we were taken from Kumbya to Bukavu, Zaire, in a van with the motor between the driver's and passenger's front seats. The van was functioning badly but the young VISA (Volunteers in Service Abroad) drivers kept it running by injecting gasoline into the motor with a tube. They dropped Myra and me at the home of a missionary who was to take us to the airport, and went on. Five minutes after leaving us the engine exploded. They were not injured and were able to save the luggage. But when Myra and I saw the charred seats where we were sitting only moments before, we lifted our hearts to God in thankfulness.

In Kinshasa the Afrolit program was similar to the original one. I was elected one of three vice-presidents. While in Kinshasa we were able to participate in tours to various places in and around the city, observing the similarities to the culture we knew in Burundi, and noting significant differences. The transforming power of the gospel was evident in many ways and places.

The second wonderful part of my 1968 trip to the U. S. was a 12-day sight-seeing visit to Israel and Europe. Three other single missionaries from Burundi, one Free Methodist and two World Gospel Mission, met me in Nairobi. From there we took a chartered tour to Israel planned and arranged by Menno Travel. About 50 missionaries made up the group and most were fun to travel with.

In Israel the important sites were either highly commercialized or partly obscured by Catholic churches or Muslim mosques. Yet it was thrilling to actually walk where Jesus walked and look at scenes he and his disciples had viewed.

In Jerusalem we stayed at a hostel within the old city wall

near the Jaffa Gate. This was just a year after the 1967 war. We were moved to see people weeping at the Wailing Wall and to walk the Via Dolorosa, a narrow street where Jesus painfully walked to Golgotha.

Of all our experiences in Jerusalem, the time spent at the Garden Tomb was the most stirring. We viewed the "Place of the Skull," the garden, and the tomb itself. The guide reminded us that the place was less important than personally knowing the risen Christ. We could easily visualize Mary's joy when Jesus met her in the garden. Our leader read the Scripture passage about this. Then we sang "Low in the grave he lay," followed by an earnest prayer. We left feeling we had truly met the living Jesus.

During our week in Israel we also visited Bethlehem and went down to Jericho and to the Dead Sea. The area of the Mountain of Temptation was so rocky and desolate, emphasizing the loneliness Jesus surely felt during his days there. I cannot relate here all the significant places we visited, nor the emotions I felt, but one of the bright spots was to dip my feet in the Sea of Galilee and cross in a small boat from Tiberias to Capernaum. Even today as I read my Bible, the places mentioned come alive as I recall the scenes I saw.

Finally we took our flight from Tel Aviv to Athens. After seeing many places of interest there, we went on to Rome. The last part of our trip took us to Switzerland where we travelled by train and by boat to Beatenburg, high in the mountains. Of course, on such a trip minor complications arose. On one flight two of the suitcases lost their handles and we had to carry them by hand about a block to the train station. But such magnificent scenery! It was worth all the effort. I shall never forget the white houses with windowboxes of red geraniums against the backdrop of the towering snow-capped mountains.

This marvelous journey added nothing to our normal air fare to fly directly to the U. S. We finally ended in New York City where we all went our separate ways. My first stop was to visit my father in Gerry Homes at Gerry, N. Y. What a joyous reunion it was! Dad's health seemed almost the same as when I had left him four years before.

After my week with dad, Harold and Sally Trevan came from Spring Arbor to take me back there to an apartment they had reserved for me. Now I faced another year of deputation ministry and felt apprehensive. What could I say to people that would be of any worth? The Lord gave me the verse: "I will be with thy mouth and will teach thee what thou shalt say" (Ex. 4:12). He kept his promise!

Once more the deputation circuit took me to New York and California, Canada and Florida, and many points in between, travelling by car, bus, train, and plane. I liked driving the best for this gave me many hours alone with the Lord. I could sing as much as I liked with no one to notice when I missed the tune! I recall one occasion when God touched my heart powerfully as I sang:

Tell me not of heavy crosses,
Nor of burdens hard to bear,
For I've found this great salvation
Makes each burden light appear!
And I love to follow Jesus,
Gladly counting all but dross,
Worldly honors all forsaking
For the glory of the cross.

Oh! the cross has wondrous beauty!
Oft I've proved this to be true.

When I'm in the way so narrow
I can see a pathway through;
And how sweetly Jesus whispers,
"Take the cross, thou needst not fear,
For I've trod this way before you
And the glory lingers near."
                    by Harriet W. Requa

Another time in my morning devotions, the Lord pointed out to me Isaiah 56:7: "They shall be joyful in the house of prayer." That evening as I spoke, the Holy Spirit filled my heart with that joy when 10 young people knelt at the altar to commit themselves to full-time service for the Lord.

When I felt weary and almost overwhelmed by the pressure of many meetings and long trips, I read Ecclesiastes 8:8 in the Berkeley version: "There's no furlough during the battle!" While my activity was called a furlough, it was actually part of the battle for the Kingdom of God. Wherever I went, the kindness and support of God's children kept me encouraged and invigorated.

I was privileged to participate in an interdenominational literature conference at Green Bay, Wisconsin, where there was a stimulating sharing of plans, projects, and ideas. Our own Mission Board also called a conference of all our Free Methodist missionaries who were involved in literature work.

Ever since the time I was hospitalized in Bujumbura with heart problems, I had occasional bouts of angina. These became rather frequent and at times severe, even after I arrived in the U. S. and was active in deputation.

It was decided that I should have a heart catheterization to determine the extent of the problem. The results were questionable. At first three doctors agreed I should have bypass surgery at once. Later they concluded the condition was not severe enough to warrant the risk. With medication I was able to continue my deputation and in due time to return to Burundi.

I saw my heart doctor shortly before returning to Africa. He said, "If it weren't that those poor beggars over there should have the Bible and you're the only one to translate it for them (I corrected that idea), I'd say you better stay in this country. But as it is, I think you'll do all right over there." While his remark showed disdain for less developed peoples, he at least realized the importance of the Bible for them.

At about the same time that I was undergoing these procedures, my father became seriously ill and was hospitalized for surgery to amputate a leg. Cancelling some of my deputation appointments, I went to be with him, but a couple days before his surgery I had to go for a weekend of meetings. As I got on a bus at 8:30 in the evening with a heavy heart, utterly weary and having some chest pain, I began to cry.

Soon it seemed as if Jesus himself came and sat beside me and said, "I love your dad, too. He's under my care." What a peace that brought! It carried me through the weekend and enabled me to give myself fully to ministry. I arrived back in Gerry at 3:00 a.m. just before my dad's surgery at 6:00. Before going to the operating room he said to me and my brother, "I have no fear at all. I'm ready to go."

Hours later he came out of the recovery room smiling and even cracked a joke! He suffered a lot in the days that followed. Once after he'd undergone an especially painful treatment, I asked him, "Did it hurt a lot?"

He replied, "You know, I've just been thinking that I have a lot to be thankful for -- it's just one leg! Think of the guys in the war that lost both legs!" You can't beat that kind of spirit!

Dad lived for another two months, much of the time in a

coma. When the call came that he was very low, I went to Gerry to be with him. He was conscious, knew me, and kept holding my hand and trying to hug me. He tried to talk but I couldn't understand him. As I sat by him for several days, my heart cried out to God, "If you love him, why don't you release him?" Once Dad raised his arm and cried out, "Home, home."

Later I was preparing some used greeting cards for Sunday school use and was writing on each one in Kirundi, "God is love." Suddenly the message came through to me, "God is love. That is his character. Everything he does flows from that." I knew then I could trust God's timing.

Three days later as I stood by Dad's side he raised his head and said, "Home! Mom!" and ceased to breathe. This tells you the kind of a dad I had. I know I shall see him again.

I was fortunate that a Free Methodist General Conference was held during my furlough. It was great to see many friends and church leaders, to observe the deliberations of our governing body, and to gain a deeper appreciation of the foundation principles of our denomination. I thanked the Lord for our godly leaders.

One of the last exciting events before my departure was the marriage of my niece Janice Cox to Gary Allen. What a delight it was to be present for that occasion! A few years later they joined me as missionaries in Burundi where they served for many years. This has brought us very close to each other.

As I prepared to return to Burundi, to my surprise our pastor's daughter, Marietta Sebree, a high school senior, decided she wanted to go with me for a six-month stay. I pointed out to her and her parents all the difficulties she might encounter. She was not deterred. It was with some trepidation that I agreed, for it is no small responsibility to serve as "mom" to a young girl for that length of time. In addition, she was not known for the depth of her spiritual life.

Before we left Spring Arbor, both of us were especially prayed for and commissioned by Pastor Sebree and others. Months later it was rewarding to hear Marietta testify that as she watched the birth of a baby she knew for sure that God is real and powerful. She said she was now committing her life to Christ in a deeper way because of what she saw in the lives of African Christians and missionaries. On one occasion, after we had a serious talk about a problem, she said, "You should have been a mom." Her kind words helped me realize the Lord had enabled me to meet the responsibility I had accepted for her.

17. These Girls

For our flight to Burundi in July 1969, Marietta and I travelled with Jim and Martha Kirkpatrick and their four young children, the best behaved youngsters on a long trip I have ever seen. On arrival Marietta was introduced to the intricacies of the red tape required in some countries. It took days of visiting several offices to get the necessary documents to go to Rwanda for the annual Kumbya missionaries' retreat. The retreat was a great time of fellowship and blessing. It felt good to again be part of a large group of people with the same goal and purpose of reaching lost people for Christ. Marietta experienced the "family" feeling that exists among missionaries of different denominations working for a common cause.

Back in my house at Kibuye, I quickly got involved again in the busy life of translation, participating in church activities, and serving on many committees, both of our own mission and of inter-mission groups. This latter aspect of my work required many trips over poor roads. I often prayed for God's protection and help as I drove.

One American visitor arrived at Kibuye and exclaimed after the drive up from Bujumbura, "Well, you can just plan to bury me here, because I'm not going on that road again!" But he did!

I had times of illness, usually my heart problem or malaria. And there were political tensions. Not long after we arrived, 20 people were executed in Bujumbura, which created much fear among our people. We were also very short on missionary personnel due to furloughs and illnesses. As a result, many extra responsibilities were added to my schedule.

One day when I was serving as mission superintendent, another single missionary and I talked with a pastor about his work. As we concluded our visit with prayer, the pastor prayed, "Lord, bless these girls. They're just girls, but in your sight they're men, and you've given them a man's work to do." In the Kirundi language there is no word for an adult unmarried lady, so though I was in my 50s, I was a "girl" in his sight!

African preachers sometimes give us a new slant on some familiar scripture story or passage. I recall one who said, "It's practically a sin to be late to church. Just think of Ananias and Sapphira. If she hadn't been late to church she would have known what happened to her husband and would have told the truth and saved her life!" (see Acts 5:1-11)

I was encouraged when our local pastor told me that some of my former students at Kibimba, now teaching at Kibuye, often asked for me to preach, and even current students home for vacation wanted me to preach while they were home. Though I have never been ordained, nor felt called specifically to preach, this was a ministry the Lord frequently gave me. I never got over my fear of speaking, yet each time as I faced a congregation the Holy Spirit took the fear away and enabled me to speak with his anointing. Also, interpreting from English to Kirundi for visiting speakers from the U.S., such as bishops, the missionary secretary and other visitors, was a frequent and challenging part of my work.

Usually our annual conferences were conducted by a visiting bishop or his appointee. Then I had to interpret both English to Kirundi and Kirundi to English as rapidly as the discussions took place. My mental powers were taxed to the limit! In later years some government official often sat in on our business meetings, I suppose to assure themselves that we were doing nothing subversive. Perhaps some gospel truths got through to them.

Sometimes a speaker didn't realize that some concepts are nearly impossible to express in an African language, or that some things and actions common in America do not exist in Africa. Thus there is no vocabulary to explain them. One bishop began his message by saying, "St. Paul was very conservative in his doctrine but progressive in his practice." I wondered, "What does he mean? How can I say this in a language that doesn't talk about *conservative* and *progressive?*" But in the fleeting moment before his next sentence I tried to convey the right idea.

Another speaker told the story of the three little pigs as an illustration, including "I'll not let you in! Not by the hair of my chinny-chin-chin!" That one really floored me! When the people spoke of trains, crackers, television, and other things the Barundi never saw or experienced, it took some ingenuity to find a suitable equivalent.

Over the years a number of Free Methodist tour groups came to visit, usually composed of 15 to 30 people. With no hotels or restaurants, finding beds and food for so many was quite a problem. But we always managed, and found we were encouraged and refreshed, too.

One Sunday evening as the missionaries shared their worship time with a tour group, one guest found Christ and another was sanctified. The long range results were often significant. As people saw the young church in action, their support, in both prayers and giving, increased greatly. Another time a man brought his family to visit and worshipped with just the few of us missionaries on a Sunday evening. Suddenly, as we were praying, this man began to pray, pouring out his heart in full commitment to Christ. He told us later he had been away from the Lord for many years.

A big undertaking at this time was a literature survey throughout the country, under the guidance of Dr. Don Smith of Daystar Communications based in Nairobi. Friends missionaries Reta Stuart and Esther Choate and I were mainly responsible for carrying it out. This involved the preparation of extensive materials, pre-testing them, training nationals to use them, frequent participation in planning committees, and working on countless other details.

Reta and I made many trips with Africans accompanying us to various parts of the country. Our purpose was to discover what kinds of literature were needed and wanted by the people, what their literacy levels were, what they believed and practiced, and how best we could make the literature ministry practical and productive. The selection of areas and individuals to be interviewed was done by the scientifically random method, and later the results were tabulated and evaluated at Daystar Communications Center. The information collected was put into a mimeographed book and became the basis for decisions regarding publication projects.

Since Rwanda and Burundi became independent in 1962, trips across the border required stops at customs offices on both sides of the border. These stops took anywhere from 15 minutes to three hours, depending on the mood or state of inebriation of the officials, or the amount of traffic that day. We never knew what to expect.

Once when Doris Moore (now Meredith), Lois Meredith and I were going to Rwanda, I was elected to take our passports to the official while the others waited in the car. As he examined our passport photos he remarked that Lois was a black and didn't really believe me when I said she was not. Then, seeing that I had an American passport and the other two were Canadian, he asked, "Why are you travelling with Canadians when Canada and America hate each other?"

On the Congo side (the road goes through a bit of Congo), the official asked for a Bible, then tried to persuade me to drink some beer with him. At the Rwanda office I was scolded because, though I knew French and Kirundi, I didn't know Kinyarwanda, which is very similar to Kirundi. In Bukavu, a provincial capital in Congo, we saw a troop of soldiers marching to the tune of "Old Folks at Home" by Stephen Foster ("Way down upon the Swanee river"). Another time as the official looked at my I.D. card, he said, "You came to Burundi in 1944? Hmm, hm, just three months after I was born!" Then, "This says you were born in 1918. That's a mistake. You can't possibly be that old!"

Quite frequently I was asked to preach in the Sunday services. On one occasion, in order to emphasize the truth that our Christianity has to be more than the veneer of verbally accepting a religion, I took a borrowed doll dressed in dirty rags. This represented our natural sinful state. Then I put on her a pretty, clean dress over the rags, and asked the congregation if she was all right now. They agreed she was not.

This led to the response, of course, that first the dirty rags must be removed. That is, our sins must be confessed and forgiven. Then the clean dress could be put on to represent the new clean life in Christ. The people's faces showed they understood that truth. After the service, everyone, including boys, wanted to touch and hold the doll. They had never seen one before. One youngster hugged and kissed it, an unusual reaction there, for people seldom kiss their children. A teenager begged me to give her the doll. The people didn't forget the message and spoke of it long afterward.

As time went on my heart problem became more severe. Often the pain was relieved only by injections of narcotics, which interfered with my work. It was finally decided that I must return to the U. S. for another evaluation, and, if necessary, undergo heart surgery. This was hard for me to accept, since I had returned from furlough only two and a half years before.

This illness was a continual, spiritual struggle for me. I prayed often for healing, and others prayed for me. Some said that healing is always possible if we have enough faith. I did much soul searching, yet the Lord did not show me any area in my life that was displeasing to him, nor did he show me how I could increase my faith. I only found peace when I fully committed the problem to him and was eager to have his will done, whatever that might be.

One Sunday a couple months before I was to leave, the Lord gave me a special experience that took away my anxiety. The night before, I lay awake a long time mulling over all I must do before departing and all that would be needed when I reached the U. S. In the morning service there came a wonderful sense of the presence of the Holy Spirit. When I got home I sat down to read a sermon by Norman Vincent Peale. He said that whenever he got tense about things, he just quoted, "Peace I leave with you. My peace I give unto you. Let not your heart be troubled."

In that moment it seemed that Jesus came and stood by me. His presence was so real! He filled my heart with his peace and joy and a deep confidence that he was in control. I hardly wanted to break from the experience to eat my dinner. It was just as if he sat down at the table with me and shared my meal. I have rarely had such a real sense of his presence.

Lois Meredith came to Kibuye to celebrate Christmas with us and help me pack all my belongings away in barrels. My translation work came to a standstill, and fellow missionaries picked up my other responsibilities. In early January I found myself back in the U. S.

After I arrived, I again heard strong preaching to the effect that we can always have healing if we have enough faith. I struggled again with how to have that kind of faith. The preacher said we should not pray, "if it's your will," for that expresses doubt. However, when I followed this reasoning I felt darkness and confusion, but when I prayed, "Lord, I only want your will and I commit this whole matter of healing to you," I felt peace and rest.

18. Tragedies And Victories

In due time another heart catheterization was performed. Again it was decided that since only minor arteries were affected, and the major ones were quite clear, surgery would be unwise. While relieved not to have to go through surgery, I was still troubled by a lot of angina pain. Many people were praying for me. One night a few days later I was awakened by severe pain. I felt the Lord say to me, "You're going to be completely well and have many more years of good healthy service." But the pain was not immediately relieved.

Then on Easter Sunday morning I got up feeling like a new person. I believed the Lord had touched me. Though there were a few tests of my faith, within a short time I was completely free of pain and had no further problem with my heart for 10 years.

Not long after my arrival in the U. S. I was visiting with my niece Janice and her husband, Gary Allen. I shared some of the needs for personnel in Burundi. A few days later they asked, "Did you tell us about the need for a teacher for missionary children in order to get us to go there?"

I replied, "No, but if that's what the Lord wants you to do, I'd be delighted." Jann was a teacher and Gary a laboratory technician. They were just three years out of college and felt they could pay their own travel to go to Burundi, but could not support themselves. We began to pray for God to make his will plain. As soon as the pastor learned of this and shared it with the official board, the Spring Arbor church agreed to support them for two years. When the matter was presented to the congregation they immediately pledged enough for their support and travel! God loves to do over and above what we ask!

The missionary secretary readily approved the Allens as VISA missionaries. They began taking French lessons from me and preparing to go to Burundi in the summer.

Then devastating news burst upon us! Massacres had begun in Burundi! The government, composed of the minority Tutsi ethnic group, feared an uprising by the majority Hutus and loosed the military to kill any Hutus with potential for leadership. Teachers, school principals, pastors, bank employees, high school students -- all were targets, along with thousands of others who had no claim to influence.

Widows and children were left with everything stripped from their homes including their gardening hoes, their means of livelihood. Our church lost about 1,000 members including five out of eight school principals, many pastors and lay ministers, the legal representative, numerous students, and many more. At one time in Gitega, our provincial capital, as many as 400 people a day were being killed and buried in mass graves by the truckload. There were threats that anyone with more than a sixth grade education would be killed. The final death toll was calculated at between 150,000 and 300,000.

How we grieved as reports came in of the loss of ones I had known or worked with! We wondered, "How can the church go on after such losses?" And what would this do to our plans to go to Burundi in a few months?

Little by little we began to hear of the amazing courage and fidelity of some of the Christians. Some were miraculously spared. Others faced the firing squad unflinchingly. There was Binyoni, school principal of a Friends school. I taught him at Kibimba and wrote about him in chapter 14. He was taken to a prison and then, along with others, taken out to be shot. As the guns were trained on them Binyoni said, "Just a minute. Could I sing first?" The soldiers looked at one another as Binyoni's clear, sweet, tenor voice rang out in Kirundi:

Out of my bondage, sorrow and night,
　　Jesus, I come, Jesus, I come;
Into thy glorious freedom and light,
　　Jesus, I come to thee.
Out of my sickness into thy health,
Out of my want and into thy wealth,
Out of my sin and into thyself,
　　Jesus, I come to thee.

Out of my shameful failure and loss,
　　Jesus, I come, Jesus, I come;
Into the glorious gain of thy cross,
　　Jesus, I come to thee.
Out of earth's sorrow into thy balm,
Out of life's storms and into thy calm,
Out of distress to jubilant psalm,
　　Jesus, I come to thee.

Out of the fear and dread of the tomb,

Jesus, I come, Jesus, I come;
Into the joy and light of thy home,
Jesus, I come to thee.
Out of the depths of ruin untold,
Into the peace of thy sheltering fold,
Ever thy glorious face to behold,
Jesus, I come to thee.

by William Sleeper

As his voice fell silent, one soldier said, "What do we do now?"

Their leader replied, "Our orders are to shoot." The guns boomed out, and Binyoni literally fulfilled the words of his song. One soldier was so moved emotionally that he went and reported this to a missionary in the city.

Another well educated man of the Friends church was a professor at Kibimba, a good friend of the local provincial governor, and also friends with a brother-in-law of the president living in Bujumbura. One morning a truck came from a neighboring province and took this professor and many other people in the area. They were forced to lie face down in the truck bed and soldiers stood on them as the truck drove on. They were taken to a prison in another town, their arms tied tightly behind them. Then they were beaten and beaten until their legs and arms were broken and they were bleeding and bruised.

Meanwhile, the missionary director of the school reported the incident to the governor. The governor told him to contact a certain man in Bujumbura, giving him the name and phone number. This was done but the man was out and not expected to return till 5:00 p.m. When he was finally located and informed of the situation, he said, "I can take care of it."

Not long after, the missionaries who had been earnestly

praying all day heard the president's helicopter go over. About an hour later they heard it return, and they wondered if their professor had been rescued. Indeed he had! The helicopter carried the head of the army who went to the prison, demanded the professor, and then announced in the name of the President that the professor and all the others taken with him were free. He ordered that they be taken back where they were picked up. Their release came just before six o'clock -- the very time they had been told they would be killed. God's timing is never too late! The professor eventually left the country and has lived in the U. S. ever since.

One of our Free Methodist pastors, Stephen, was also picked up and thrown onto a truck along with many others. As they went along he began to sing a hymn. A soldier near him said, "What are you singing for? Don't you know you're about to be killed?"

"Yes," answered Stephen, "I know. That's why I'm singing. I'll soon be where nothing can ever hurt me again. You can only kill me. But if you do, I'll be with my wonderful Jesus for- ever."

The truck soon stopped and some of the people were allowed to get off under heavy guard. This same soldier edged Stephen off to the margin of the crowd, then pushed him, say- ing, "Go, run, get out of the country."

Stephen did that and escaped to Zaire where he served the church and gave radiant testimony. Four years later he felt God told him to return to Burundi. He obeyed, though it seemed foolhardy, for some returning refugees had been imprisoned. He again pastored the Muyebe church until the present time, and God has given him a most fruitful ministry.

After the mass killings the government ordered that no one was to help the many widows. They were penniless and were stripped of everything. One of our pastors who was a Tutsi, thus unharmed, would get up in the night and take hoes to several widows, then help them find a little plot to cultivate and plant a few sweet potatoes. In the morning before daylight he would collect the hoes and hide them. He was risking his own life in doing this, but God's love prevailed.

Back in Michigan we were praying night and day for the situation, watching for every bit of news and praying about our future in relation to it all. A report came that no new visas were being granted. Those who left the country before all these events began would have to re-apply for entry. At the same time, I was receiving letters from our missionaries urging me to come back as soon as possible. The Missionary Secretary said I could not go back before November. Knowing God was in control and believing he would work out his will, we continued our preparation to go to Burundi.

While watching developments I continued my deputation ministry, speaking many times in several camps. The Lord helped me, and I'm sure many people were stirred up to pray for Burundi as never before. I arrived at one camp late in the day, weary from a heavy week of ministry. One lady met me on the path and asked, "Who are you?" When she heard my name, recognizing that I was their missionary speaker, she looked me up and down, and said, "My! The years have surely taken their toll on you!" I returned to my room chuckling. She had never seen me before, but I must have looked pretty bad.

Finally arriving back home, I learned that the Allens had gotten their visa without difficulty and were booked to fly to Burundi August 29.

I went to Winona Lake, Indiana, for a week of orientation for missionaries returning for furlough, but first I had an interview with Dr. Kirkpatrick, Missionary Secretary. I was delighted when he said I could go back to Burundi as soon as it could be arranged. I replied, "Like on August 29 with the Allens?" (This was August 21!)

He said, "I don't see why not if you can get ready and if a reservation can be made."

Wow! That sort of took my breath away. My barrels were already packed, and by the next morning I had my reservation to fly to Bujumbura with the Allens. Instead of attending the orientation seminar, I was preparing to leave in just one week for another term in Burundi!

No one in Burundi knew I was coming. They were expecting the Allens so a nice group was at the airport to meet them. As we walked a short distance from the plane to the terminal it was fun to hear astonished voices shouting, "There's Betty Ellen!"

Jann's first personal encounter with an African was with a national dentist the afternoon after our arrival. A tooth had troubled her on the journey. He did a good job.

As we neared Kibuye with two of our missionaries from there, children along the road saw me (travel was slow on our poor roads) and began to shout, "Kagisi karaje!" (Cox has come!) What a warm welcome I received from both missionaries and Barundi!

It felt good to be back. Yet my heart ached as I learned of one person after another whose life had been taken. Fear filled many hearts and homes, and there was much deprivation and sorrow and suffering. Over and over people thanked me for coming in spite of the conditions. The end of the killing had not yet come. I wasn't there long when I helped save one man's life. He was twice called to the local government office, but because I went with him, they didn't do anything. But soon after he was taken away to prison. I was able to get the right wheels turning so he was released before any harm came to him. Many times afterward he expressed his thanks to me and to God.

Among the Barundi who came to welcome me was Suzana, now a widow with seven children. She told how, after her husband was killed, the soldiers came and took her chickens, goats, cooking pots, hoe and nearly everything else. She concluded with a smile, "But I'm so much better off than many others! I have Jesus, and they don't have anybody."

When our local pastor greeted me on my arrival, he said, "Thank God you've come back to give us more literature! During these past troubles, people kept coming to church, but they were so exhausted from fear and sorrow that they could scarcely hear what the preachers were saying. But they were reading the Bible as never before (the Bible had been in their language only four years). Oh, thank God we got the whole Bible before this awful thing happened!"

19. Massacres And Marriages

I was soon back into my regular routine. No, not quite the *regular* one. For one thing, I was asked to teach French at Mweya (an hour's drive away) to third year seminary students. I was reluctant to do this, for my real desire was to concentrate on the literature work. To teach at Mweya would take the best part of two days each week, with preparation and correction of written work, plus travel counted in. Yet as I prayed about it, I became convinced that God wanted me to do it so I agreed.

I learned some interesting things from the French class:

(1) The reason it's necessary to make tight joints when constructing a table or chair is to keep the bedbugs out.

(2) For successful fishing a person must have the right kind of "medicine" to put into the water, never sit on the bank of the river, and never eat manioc before fishing!

(3) When I said that one part of honesty (for which there is no word in Kirundi) is to always tell the truth, I was told, "Then there is no such thing in the world as an honest person,

because no one always tells the truth."

Perhaps the greatest benefit of the French teaching was that Noah Nzeyimana became one of my literature assistants after his graduation and continued very efficiently in that capacity for five years. Noah, Joseph and I made a good team, each one using his special abilities.

The other thing that was not "the regular routine" was the aftermath of the events of 1972. People continued to be arrested, or to disappear. The sufferings and penury of widows and orphans were appalling. Even some widows were arrested, leaving young children orphans.

All the Swedish Pentecostal missionaries were expelled from the country which made us all feel that our situation was tenuous. However, a few years later they were allowed to return. Sometimes political rallies were held and we were ordered to attend. At one, churches were ordered not to count widows and orphans or to give them clothes or other aid. They said foreigners were welcome if they worked for the country, not against it. We were told not to visit people in their homes. The government announced by radio that if any refugee had not returned by November 1972 his property would be confiscated and given to someone else.

One Christian man, seized and thrown on the back of a truck with a crowd of others, was sure they were all on their way to execution. As they went along, he saw a friend walking beside the road and shouted to him, "Hey, I'm going to beat you to heaven." Then they were all unloaded from the truck and shoved into a little cell, packed in. But he had slipped a gospel into his pocket, so while they stood awaiting their death, he read to them and led several to Christ. After a time, a soldier opened the door and told them to go home. No one knew why their lives were spared but he went all around testifying of God's mighty grace that first saved his soul, then later his life.

With the loss of so many of our people, we again wondered, *Can the church possibly go on*? But even when Satan does his worst, God still wins in the end. At annual conference in 1973 a memorial service was held for the six pastors killed the year before, and prayer was offered for the people still suffering from the effects of the massacres. We were deeply stirred to see how God was calling others to rise up and carry on the work, and to hear of their determination and hope for the future. One pastor gave this testimony:

"I was thrown into a cell all alone so I decided I'd better have a talk with Jesus. I said, 'Jesus, you see me here, and you see what has happened to me. I think you'd better go talk to the governor about me.' So that's just what he did. He went and told the governor, 'That man is in a cell in such and such a place. You set him free.' The governor quickly sent someone who came and opened the door of my cell. He told me to go home so I did."

Actually, this man pastored at Rutunga, one of our most progressive outstations. They built their own church, an eight-classroom school, and a dispensary in faith that a nurse would be sent to them. When the tragedy of 1972 struck and passed over that area, there was absolutely no one left. All had been killed or had fled to another country across the lake. The buildings had been looted and damaged. It looked like the end for Rutunga. But gradually the people began to drift back, and this pastor resumed his work among them.

At Christmas time (1972) he got permission from the officials to hold a Christmas service. Their church had lost its windows, doors, and benches, but on Christmas morning the little congregation sat huddled on the dirt floor. Their pastor began to tell them the beautiful old story of God coming to earth because of love. Suddenly a soldier burst in, grabbed the pastor, dragged him outside, beat him up, then took him away and shoved him into a cell.

The pastor was released and reported at conference that he would go right back to Rutunga to continue to serve the Jesus he loved. A year later I heard the district superintendent say, "All last year I'd go to Rutunga and see the devastation and ruin, and the tears would flow. But last week my heart was filled with joy and praise. When I went back to Rutunga the little church was filled with people singing the praises of God. There were still no windows or doors or benches, but the people were worshipping God and rejoicing." Jesus said, "I will build my church."

In January of 1973 the rains were excessively heavy and the crops were being damaged. Local officials locked up all the rain-makers of the area -- men who say they can cause it to rain or stop raining. When my cook told me about this I laughed, but he looked at me very seriously and said, "Mademoiselle, this is no laughing matter." I realized again how wide the gap is between our western culture and theirs. Strangely enough, it did not rain again for two or three weeks! I really can't explain that.

April of that year was a very full and important month. First, the Central Africa Fellowship Conference met in Bukavu, Zaire, for four days. This conference serves Zaire, Rwanda, and Burundi, and meets once every four or five years. I was asked to participate in order to interpret all the messages and transactions into Kirundi. There were 12 church leaders from America and a number of delegates from Zaire and Rwanda (all of these delegates understood Kirundi), but none were there from Burundi, due to the political tensions.

It was a time of inspiration, fellowship, and planning for the future. The meeting served its purpose well by bringing Free Methodists of these areas into a closer understanding of one another and uniting them in a common goal of reaching lost people for Christ. Another important event that month was the Burundi annual conference.

But the really big event that month was the wedding in Bujumbura of Miriam Wheeler (a nurse in Burundi) and Irvin Cobb (a teacher in Rwanda). They met while studying French in Belgium, a requirement for all medical and educational missionaries in those countries.

Missionary weddings are rare overseas so everyone wanted to be a part of it. The ceremony was a beautiful service on a private lawn with a backdrop of Lake Tanganyika and surrounded by lovely flowers. Their ministry together in Rwanda was blessed and used of God until they had to retire in 1989 due to Miriam's health problems. They have three handsome sons who are all serving the Lord.

Another missionary nurse, Priscilla Osborne, came to Burundi with Miriam Wheeler. Both Miriam and Priscilla worked in the hospital. It was my privilege to teach them the language, so we had grown very fond of each other.

After Miriam's marriage she and Irvin went to work in Rwanda. Now, a year later, Priscilla began to tell us of her own wedding plans. At our Kumbya retreat she met Nate Thompson, a VISA missionary in Zaire whose specialty was mechanics. They sensed God leading them to a life together. April 1974 was a busy time as preparations were made for their wedding in the Kibuye church. One WGM missionary made a gorgeous cake, Jann Allen made lovely corsages, and many of us prepared special foods for the rehearsal dinner and wedding lunch.

I was honored to stand in as the bride's mother at the request of Pris's mother. The wedding was as beautiful as any in an American church. Pris and Nate served effectively in three central African countries. They have a son and daughter who are serving the Lord.

* * * * * * * * *

A couple months after the Cobb wedding, the Allens and I made a trip to East Africa with other missionaries. As always, it was a thrill to visit the game parks in Kenya and Tanzania and see wild animals of every kind. At one time a rhinoceros was coming down the road right toward us (they're quite short-sighted). We stopped but he didn't -- until just a few feet from us he veered off. We also went down into beautiful Ngorongoro Crater, teeming with animals and birds, one of nature's marvels.

In Nairobi I was thrilled to learn that Carolyn Winslow was staying at the same guest house as we were. A missionary to China, Carolyn was one of the godliest people I have known. She was my "ideal" from the time she was one of my high school teachers.

Now, of all times, she was en route to visit our work in Burundi just when I could not be there! But we were able to spend several hours together before she left. Her impact on my life across the years has been greater than that of almost anyone else. What a blessing it has been to have known Carolyn!

Another delightful part of that trip was to drive on to Mombasa and spend a couple days at the coast on the Indian

Ocean, a most beautiful tropical scene. Restful times like this renewed our energies and our spirits. How graciously the Lord provides for us just what he sees we need!

On my return I had to assume the duties of mission superintendent since the Kirkpatricks had left for furlough. I was elected to that office since the other missionaries were relatively new to the work. There were always business letters to be written in English or French or Kirundi -- very time consuming. At times I felt overwhelmed by these responsibilities, knowing that I was not sufficiently capable, but I learned to rely on the Lord for his guidance and enabling. Once when there was a problem in my accounts that I couldn't solve I asked the Lord for help and went to bed. In the middle of the night I awakened with the solution perfectly clear to me.

The work of superintendent required a lot more time on the road to attend committee meetings, make government contacts, and settle matters relating to the other missionaries or other missions. In fact, in 1974 I was away from home all or part of 142 days, mostly on mission business.

Once when I began the drive from Bujumbura to Kibuye, I realized there was a problem with the gears on the car. On that road, within the first 25 miles, the altitude rises from 2,500 feet to about 7,000. I found that I could only shift into second gear, and that with much difficulty, but I kept going for there was no place to stop or get repairs. Suddenly a roadblock appeared where road work was going on. I had to stop completely.

I was in trouble. When the workers motioned for me to go on, I struggled to shift into low but could not. Finally I managed to start up the hill in second, and just kept going for 60 more miles to Mweya. There, when the car was examined, they found I had driven all that way with a broken clutch cable!

In addition to my travels, for years I taught a Sunday school class of teenage girls whom I felt were rather unresponsive. One Sunday as I talked about Jesus' crucifixion I saw some of them rubbing the palms of their hands, obviously empathizing with Jesus' pain. Soon after one of them testified that she repented of her sins and gave her heart to Jesus. A few days later, six of them came to my home to ask me to pray for them. In the revival that began soon after, eight others came to Christ. It paid to hang in there all those years when I wondered whether anything I said was getting through to them.

Nationals were being trained for Sunday school and youth ministries, and most of the Sunday schools were taught and administered by them. Once, at the close of Sunday school, the leader said, "We'll now have the secretary's report." The secretary quite importantly mounted the platform with a sheaf of papers in his hand. Here is his complete report: "It went well in Sunday school today, but not very well."

We had plenty of lighter moments. Before making a trip to Rwanda I went to the police office to apply for an international driver's license. These countries don't recognize one another's legal documents. The conversation went like this:

B.E.:   I wish to apply for an international driver's license.
Officer: Have you ever had one before?
B.E.:   Yes, but it expired a long time ago so I destroyed it.
Officer: You go and get your former license and we'll issue you a new one.
B.E.:   I'm sorry I can't do that. I destroyed the old one; burned it up.
Officer: You go and get it . . . .

(This dialogue was repeated four or five times.)

Officer: Well, the facts are we don't have any forms for an
international license.

So I went on, hoping that Rwanda would accept my U. S.
license.

20. How Do Churches Grow?

One of the thrills of working in Burundi was watching how the Lord developed his church. In the early days most leadership, training, preaching were in the hands of missionaries. In later years all the school principals were nationals, as were the pastors and district superintendents. Missionaries preached only occasionally on the invitation of the pastors. Business meetings also were capably led by the Barundi themselves.

In 1974 an inter-mission church-growth seminar was held with specialists in church growth from America speaking. At one point the attendees were asked to separate into their various denominational groups and set five-year goals for new church plants and membership gains. I was present only as interpreter for the guest speakers but was invited to sit in with the Free Methodist group.

The pastors and laymen began to discuss what goals they should set. They got more and more excited about what God was doing in various places and what they expected him to do in the coming years. Thinking of the preceding years, I was astounded when the gains they wanted to set seemed utterly unreasonable and impossible. I bit my lips to keep from protesting as I envisaged their disappointment when their goals were not met.

Three years later (not five), they reached all those goals, both in the number of new churches and in new members. How glad I was that this woman of little faith had kept still instead of dampening their enthusiasm!

Often in America we are asked, "How do you account for the rapid church growth in that part of the world?" Part of my answer is that the church has many lay ministers. They often support themselves while ministering out on the hills away from the centers, preaching and teaching and leading people to Jesus. Most of them have had a little training through TEE (Theological Education by Extension). TEE is composed of courses with instruction and questions to which they write answers, meeting weekly with a leader to discuss them. It has been my privilege to translate from English many of the books used for this study in both Burundi and Rwanda.

The dense population of these regions is also a contributing factor to the large response to the gospel. But in the final analysis, the Holy Spirit at work in and through people's lives is the one who produces the growth.

The three holiness missions (Friends, World Gospel Mission, and Free Methodist) decided the TEE program would be practical for Bible training for pastors and lay ministers. Africans could take these courses while continuing their pastoral ministry. Our literature team was asked to translate and mimeograph materials prepared in English specifically for use in Africa. The first book completed was *The Shepherd and His Work,* written in South Africa by Free Methodists Don

Crider and Seth Msweli.

One Friends' outschool was badly deteriorated. They no longer had a pastor nor held services. Only a primary school with a backslidden director continued to function. Someone persuaded him to study this book. When he turned to the first page he read, "You are an example to your people."

He thought, "What kind of an example am I -- drinking, smoking, lying, stealing and all the rest?" The Holy Spirit struck conviction to his heart. He fell to his knees and began to repent. Soon he found peace. A few days later he announced that there would be a church service even without a pastor. The people came and the director stood up and simply told what Jesus had done for him. The altar filled with seekers. The church was revived and soon began to grow.

In many places pastors began to have a more effective ministry. Their work was better organized, they had clear goals, and they had a definite purpose in their sermons. The wives of pastors, too, were affected by the influence of the book and began to share more in their husbands' work. Some said, "We want to take this course, too, for we've seen such a wonderful change in our husbands."

Even people not in ministry became interested and were changed by the study. Domina came from a Catholic family, was working at the Catholic mission, but had begun at times to attend church at Kibuye. One day Noah showed her the TEE book and she got quite excited about learning more about the Bible. She faithfully studied the lessons, wrote the answers, and walked in the light of them even though she was unable to attend the group session because of her work. Finally the priest called her in. She was frightened but went singing.

The priest said, "I haven't seen you in mass lately. Where

have you been?"

"I've been going to church at Kibuye," she replied.

"Why do you go there?" was the next question.

"Because I'm learning about the Bible. I want to know it better."

He asked, "What are you learning about the Bible?"

For her answer she opened her TEE book to a page that explained the steps necessary to know you are saved. She handed it to him.

After looking it over a bit, the priest said, "This sounds all right. Do you believe it?"

"Believe it? Of course I do," she exclaimed, "because it has happened to me!"

Then getting up her courage, she said, "The only trouble is I can't go to the class where they discuss this because of my work."

"Be careful," admonished the priest, "you might get sick in the head if you study this kind of thing too much. But if you want to go enough to take a cut in pay, we could let you off."

"Wonderful!" Domina exclaimed, "the pay doesn't matter! All that matters is learning more about the Bible."

Slowly came the priest's answer: "I'm going to give you five months notice. During that time you will have to make a choice between your job and this study."

Without hesitation Domina answered, "You don't need to give me five months! I've already made my choice. Jesus is so precious to me that if it means my job, that's all right." She lost her job but later was given work at Kibuye hospital.

Church members and attendees were learning to practice the principles of Christian living. A young boy, seeking the Lord, was asked, "Why did you go to the altar?"

He replied, "I wanted to be saved because I didn't like the

way I was." Two weeks later he brought six friends to Sunday school and church.

Kosiya was my cook during my first six years on the field at Kibuye. At that time he was a Christian, but later he drifted away from the Lord and became dark and sullen. For about 20 years he seemed to have no interest in church and had a negative influence on his family. But one day during revival meetings he came to a service, obviously with his mind made up to return to the Lord. After a short time of prayer he arose with the light of joy on his face replacing the sullenness. From that time on he rarely missed a service and always had a smile. This is the work of the Holy Spirit.

One year people were suffering hunger because of failed crops. Then on a Saturday afternoon there came a hail storm so severe that it even killed cows. What few crops they had were totally destroyed. The hail even penetrated the ground and stripped the sweet potatoes.

The next day Twaha, my literature assistant, was to lead singing at church. He told of the hail storm, then said, "Last night my family went to bed without any supper. There was absolutely nothing left to eat." Then he read Romans 8:35-39: "Who shall separate us from the love of Christ? Shall troubles, or disasters, or hunger? No, in all these things we are made to conquer more and more by the one who loved us. For I know beyond any doubting that neither death nor life nor anything else shall be able to separate us from the love of God." (I've translated the Kirundi version back to English.) He followed that passage by leading the congregation in singing, "I have decided to follow Jesus, no turning back, no turning back."

Without being prompted, when the people came to the next prayer meeting and for several weeks afterward, those who came from areas not hit by the hail brought little baskets of dry beans to give to those who had lost everything.

After the storm destroyed almost everything, huge insects came and began to devour the bit of grass that escaped the hail. Twaha prayed for God to take them away. In a couple of days big flocks of crows came and ate up all the insects. Shortly not one was left, and Twaha knew that God had heard his prayer.

For several years Radio Cordac, our evangelical Protestant broadcasting station, sent forth the gospel in several languages. During a time of political tensions in the country, one day a government official walked into the offices of Cordac and ordered the director to turn off the transmitters at once. No explanation was given.

At the same time the Claytons' visa was due to be renewed routinely, but when application was made it was refused and they were given 48 hours to leave the country. Howard Clayton was Cordac's only technician. Two other couples applied for visas to come to work for Cordac and were refused.

When Cordac's staff began their weekly prayer meeting, the Director, Tim Kirkpatrick, brother of Jim, read I Thessalonians 5:18: "In everything give thanks, for this is the will of God in Christ Jesus concerning you."

"Now," he said, "we are going to obey that command, for it is a command. So let us begin by thanking God that Cordac is off the air."

They rather feebly sang their little praise chorus, "May Jesus be praised."

Then he said, "Let's praise God now that Claytons have to leave day after tomorrow." An African staff member jumped to his feet shouting, "Stop it! How can we thank God for things like this? This can't be God's will!"

"But," said Tim, "the Bible says 'in everything'." So they sang their chorus of praise. "Now let's thank God that visas have been denied for those two couples." They did, a bit stronger this time.

"And now," the director took a deep breath, "let's thank God that we haven't been able to get permission for the last five years to use the new 10kw transmitter that lies in the warehouse."

That *was* a big one. But the praise rang out.

One week later the staff met to pray again. Cordac was back on the air (the day following the previous prayer meeting). The Claytons had a one-year visa (as long as is ever issued). Visas had been granted for the two couples, and one couple was already in the air on the way. And, wonder of wonders, permission had finally been granted to use the 10kw transmitter! All because of praise! Why don't we use this method more often?

21. Renewal

A special privilege was mine in the summer of 1975. I took a six-week course in Communications at Daystar University in Nairobi directed by Dr. Don Smith who had guided us in our Literature Survey. The courses were interesting and challenging, and I acquired some practical material along with a very satisfactory grade.

One weekend during the course students were lodged in African homes with people of a culture different from their own. I was placed in a Christian Kikamba home. The family all knew English, and the home furnishings were quite European. They had great fun teaching me some of their language and were quite hilarious when I recognized the meaning of some of their words because of their similarity to Kirundi. Since they got so much fun out of my visit they decided to give me a new name: *Ndanu* meaning Happiness.

Worshipping with the Wakamba on Sunday was fascinating. At the time of the offering some people gave produce. The produce was auctioned off to the highest bidder accompanied by a lot of fun and laughter. This method significantly increased the amount of the offering. Even so, I'm not sure I'd recommend it as a general practice.

After the course I stayed on in Nairobi for 10 days of vacation and to get some dental work done. Then I flew back to Rwanda just in time for our annual Kumbya missionaries' retreat, which again provided a time of renewal and recharging spiritual batteries.

Back home, after a two months absence, I was inundated with catching up on translation work, participating in various committees in different locations, teaching my Sunday school class, and taking an occasional turn at preaching on Sunday morning. Various extras also came along: giving Alliance language exams to missionaries of various denominations and helping Victor Macy find personnel and settings for a film he was making. The film turned out great, and I had the privilege of getting acquainted with the Macys.

The Lord was working in my own heart even while I was seeking to help others. Often as I translated, some special sentence or phrase would penetrate my thinking in a particular way. One day we had just translated, "I was bad and there had to be a punishment, but God looked at me and loved me, so he said, *I'll take her punishment!*"

Think of it! The Almighty God taking *my* punishment! I had known that all my life but it struck a chord in my heart that day. Some days later, Josephine, a young earnest Christian, came to pour her heart out to me, telling of her ups and downs and times of discouragement.

Afterward I thought, "What Josephine needs is holiness, real victory through the Holy Spirit," but I hadn't talked to her about it. Then as I began preparing my sermon for the following Sunday, I felt led to preach about holiness. I searched for a good modern example in books such as *I Met a Man with a Shining Face* and *Samuel Brengle*. As I did so, I realized that my own experience of holiness was mostly something that happened a long time ago. I saw how full of self I was, concerned with my own rights and with what people think of me.

Suddenly I was pouring this all out to God in confession and surrendering myself anew to him. Immediately the Holy Spirit came in cleansing, renewing power. All alone in the house I shouted and wept and felt completely made new. I had been so dried up and empty, and powerless when I tried to help people. Now this fresh touch from God put everything in a new light. Across the years, from time to time, the Holy Spirit has taken control of my life in a new invigorating, empowering way. How thankful I am for this!

The greatest reward for my efforts came in seeing lives truly changed by Jesus coming into their hearts. Some found Jesus while children, others as adults. Each summer a VBS (Vacation Bible School) was held in many of our churches. Lois Meredith often directed these and trained teachers for them. One year at Kibuye, Faustin, an elementary school teacher and a refugee from Rwanda, attended VBS along with the children. Whatever the children did -- coloring pictures, memorizing Scripture, the whole of it -- Faustin did with them.

Lois remarked to me that she wasn't sure why he was there since there were no other adults besides the teachers. But on the final day when the invitation was given to receive Jesus into their hearts, Faustin knelt at the altar along with the children and gave himself to Christ. A few days later he went to Twaha in the bookstore and said, "I don't know very much yet about being a Christian so if you see me doing anything I shouldn't, please tell me."

Faustin and his wife began to visit me in my home and I returned the visits, praying that God would establish them in the faith. Two or three years later I was asked to re-write the *Kirundi Grammar* for Kinyarwanda since the two languages are very similar. Needing a Rwandan national to assist me, I asked Faustin if he could help. He readily agreed. As we worked side by side I began to notice the smell of tobacco on him. I felt the Holy Spirit leading me to speak about it so I asked, "Do you smoke?"

"Yes, I've tried and tried to quit, but I just can't."

"You know Jesus could help you if you'd ask him to."

"Could he really? Could we pray about it now?" So we each prayed a short prayer asking for his deliverance.

A few days later I asked Faustin, "How are you getting along?"

"Just fine!" he said. "The only time I have any desire for tobacco is when the baby cries at night and wakes me. But I threw all my cigarettes away that first day we prayed so it's no problem."

Some weeks later I wanted to pay him for his work on the Grammar. He said, "I couldn't possibly take any pay. The deliverance from tobacco is worth far more than anything you could pay me!"

Sometimes in our conversations I mentioned to Faustin the great concern I felt for teenagers in our congregation. After elementary school they had almost no opportunities. Most could not go on to secondary school because too few schools on that level existed in the country, and only the very brightest were accepted for the few available places. Not many job opportunities existed either, and just helping cultivate their parents' fields wasn't very promising. Faustin began to share my concern for these young folks.

* * * * * * * *

Great sorrow comes into the lives of all of us at times. Missionaries are not exempt. One Saturday morning while I was in Gitega chairing a meeting of the Gitega Literature Center Board, the phone rang with a call for Jim Kirkpatrick. We were all overcome with shock to learn that his 14-year-old daughter, Beth, had just died. She was staying for the weekend with an aunt and her family at Nyakarago. Beth and her cousin were climbing among some rocks beside a waterfall when she suddenly fell, tumbling over the rocks and into the water, breaking her neck.

The cousin quickly called her father who came and carried Beth to the house. He tried to give her artificial respiration all the way, but her life was gone. Jim went at once to Mweya to share the sad news with Martha and their other children. They decided that Beth would be buried at Kibuye beside Berdina Beckwith and that the funeral would be Sunday afternoon.

Doris Moore (Meredith) was away in Rwanda, so I was the only regular missionary at Kibuye, but Harold and Lorena Truax and Earl Terman (VISA missionaries) were there doing construction work at the hospital. All the responsibility for arrangements and preparations rested on me.

On my way home I stopped at the local official's residence to get permission for the burial and funeral -- a miracle to find him home on Saturday afternoon! Since many of the mission stations of various denominations have short-wave radio transmitters, the news was quickly disseminated throughout the country.

All the responsibility for arrangements and preparations for Beth Kirkpatrick's funeral rested on me. Since many of the mission stations of various denominations have short-wave radio transmitters, the news was quickly disseminated throughout the country. It was astonishing to see the ready response of the missionaries of all groups.

Seeing the ready response of the missionaries of all groups was astonishing. A Friends mechanic came at once to repair our broken-down generator so we could have electricity. A WGM nurse, Betty Schultz, came and offered to help me and stayed overnight. A WGM man brought three cases of Coca-Cola to serve with refreshments after the funeral. Lorena made up beds in the guest house for the Kirkpatrick family. I cut all the flowers I could find and Betty and I spent the evening making a wreath and a spray of flowers. Meanwhile, Harold and Earl dug the grave. All this time we were hurting and weeping for Jim and Martha and their other children. It all seemed so unreal.

Sunday morning I learned by radio that 10 or so people would be here for dinner before the funeral, so we prepared for a dozen. But people kept coming. As we began to serve the plates of food the supply was always enough for one or two more. When all were served I counted the plates used (no paper plates here), and 35 people had shared adequately from that dinner for 12 -- another miracle of "multiplying the loaves!"

The WGM mission provided refreshments to serve after the funeral to the 150-200 friends who had come. Others brought beautiful floral arrangements as lovely as any florist in the United States could have prepared. God's provision was also evident in that they had found in Bujumbura the only casket in the country. It was a lovely one. Two ladies had prepared Beth for burial even before Jim and Martha reached their home in Bujumbura.

The Lord gave marvelous grace and peace to the Kirkpatrick family. Just the night before Beth's accident she told her young cousin some of her favorite Bible verses and said, "If I should die, I'm ready to meet Jesus." The funeral service was beautiful with Gerald Bates speaking and Jim Morris (Friends) giving a tribute. I interpreted all this and the obituary into Kirundi for the Africans who were present and sorrowing with us. A wonderful sense of the presence of Jesus was evident and the assurance was given that God's will had been accomplished in Beth's brief life.

22. The Lost Is Found

The construction of the new hospital building required quite a bit of my time. I interpreted for the VISA missionaries and their workmen, helped order supplies, fed the missionaries, drew copies of the hospital plans, handled finances, and was frequently called on to answer questions or interpret for someone. But seeing the badly needed building take form and visualizing its future usefulness made it all worthwhile.

The hospital had needed a doctor for a couple years. For long periods Doris Moore and I were the only missionaries living at Kibuye. An appeal for a doctor to meet this need was put in *Light and Life* magazine. The only one who responded was dear Dr. Kuhn, then in her 70s, who had been retired for some time. She arrived in April 1976 and came to live with me. Arthritis made it difficult for her to get around, but she was as sharp as ever in her medical abilities.

About this time Pris and Nate Thompson came back to Kibuye along with their daughter Cerissa, who celebrated her first birthday at my house just after they arrived. When she saw the cake with its one candle, before anyone could stop her, she grabbed the flame! Fortunately, she wasn't burned. Now Cerissa is a young lady graduating from Greenville College. Many missionaries were coming and going almost daily for medical, construction, or other reasons, so while it was good to have fellowship with them, much time was spent in socializing.

I was asked to be the speaker for a women's conference at Ngagara, near Bujumbura. Though it was hard to find time to prepare my messages, the Lord helped me. How wonderfully he fills in where we lack! Some 400 women were in attendance for the three-day meetings. About 60 of them sought the Lord during those days. In the Sunday morning service another 16 or so people sought the Lord, most of these young men.

In June I received word from Mission Headquarters that I was to go on furlough in July. Earlier they told me I could not go until December because of a shortage of funds. It would be a rush to get ready in time, for furloughing involves a lot more than simply packing a suitcase and taking off.

My various responsibilities, including some inter-mission ones, would have to be turned over to others with all accounts put in order and audited. Files of business matters had to be sorted, current translation projects completed, and all my belongings packed away in barrels, except for enough supplies for Dr. Kuhn to use for the remainder of her time there. In the meantime Sally Trevan in Spring Arbor began searching for an apartment and car for me. What a dear friend she is!

The time flew by and I soon found myself returning to the U. S. for my sixth furlough. The goodbyes and readjustments to a different culture are not easy, both when we leave and when we come back. In fact, we never know on departure whether we will ever return to that place again.

On the plane flying over Europe in late evening, high above the clouds, we could occasionally see a peak of the Alps poking up through, touched by the setting sun. Beside us a jet trail glowed silver for perhaps 100 miles with the tiniest line of a crescent moon just above it. Simply gorgeous! As our plane flew straight as an arrow on an apparently unmarked path with no landmarks to guide, I thought of how God guides our lives just as surely in a way where we cannot see any markers. But he knows the way and guides unerringly. I'm content to simply follow him and glad I can trust my life to his unfailing care.

A group of friends met me at the Detroit airport, and shortly we were headed for Spring Arbor. In Jackson we stopped at Loud's famous ice cream parlour. Coming from a country where many people are hungry or poorly nourished, I stepped into that room where many apparently overweight people sat consuming enormous mounds of ice cream. I was almost overwhelmed at the contrast.

Very soon I was installed in a cute little house known as "The Doll House" which Sally had reserved for me. Wilbur Williamson loaned me a used Buick Skylark to be mine throughout the furlough. God's people are so kind and caring!

Furlough meant the usual round of medical check-ups, replenishing the wardrobe, and travelling across the country to speak in many churches. It also included the joy of reunion with family and friends in various parts of the country. How precious it is to be part of the family of God!

We were leaving the service after one Missionary Celebration in which a particularly moving message (not by me) had been given. I heard one lady say in frustration, "I can't stand to hear any more of this heart-rending stuff, especially when there's nothing we can do about it!"

I couldn't help thinking, *Dear friend, how much do you pray about these heart-rending situations? In the midst of your abundance and ease, is it too painful to hear of those who have nothing or are suffering?*

In most of my services I have a table of artifacts neatly labelled to give a little insight to the culture of the country I served in. In one place, a group of CYC youngsters came into the sanctuary early and were looking at the artifacts. One boy picked up an antelope horn on which the label said that a witchdoctor had used it. The boy asked me, "How did the witchdoctor use it?"

I gave him a demonstration. Then he asked, "But how did you get it?"

I replied, "A witchdoctor got saved and he gave it to me."

He ran back to the other kids and shouted, "Hey, listen you guys! A witchdoctor got saved! Ain't that neat?"

One of the highlights of this furlough was the privilege of spending time with Carolyn Winslow. She had now retired in Spring Arbor. Since my high school days she has been sort of my "ideal." She was such a godly woman, a woman of prayer and faith, thinking of others before herself, always reaching out to people to draw them to Jesus. At times she invited me to a meal with her or we sat together in church when I was in Spring Arbor. At other times, I took her to the airport or to town for business. Once she inadvertently let me know that her "tithe" was 40% of her income. My life has been greatly enriched by Carolyn.

When I was the missions speaker at a Maryland camp, I was able to spend some time with my niece Karyl Garn and her family who lived near there. During this time Karyl renewed her commitment to the Lord and has been faithfully walking with him ever since. One of the few sacrifices in a missionary's life is having so little contact with family and relatives, so these times with them are especially precious.

The furlough summer was filled with camps in various parts of the country. At the Cattaraugus camp in New York they had two nice little cottages side by side, one for the missionary speaker(s), and one for the evangelist. The LeRoy Kettinger family occupied the cottage next to me.

I returned to my cottage with a friend after an afternoon meeting and we sat on the porch and chatted. Soon we noted the Kettingers were searching for their five-year-old son. The camp was alerted and people looked everywhere for the boy. When my visiting friend left I went into my cottage. And there lay the missing boy sound asleep on my couch!

At the camps I particularly enjoyed my contacts with the children and youth. It was raining one day as I talked to the children, making it hard to hear. As I finished it rained harder so they couldn't dismiss the children. One girl came to me and said, "Maybe God made it rain so you'd tell us more stories."

A couple days later, after I spoke to the youth group, a young man about 18 years old came to talk at my cottage. After a short chat he accepted Christ as his Savior. As he left, an old man came to see me and handed me a check for $1,000 for my work. I was astonished. I had never before received a gift of that size, but I thanked him and the Lord for it. That would buy a new mimeograph machine that I had hoped to get for my work in Burundi.

My next camp was quite a small one and interest in missions seemed at a low ebb. Each day I spoke to a small group at a missions service and had brief "missions moments" in

The clerk at Gitega Literature Center and Bookstore is telling me it's time to order more copies of the *Kirundi Grammar* and *Dictionary*, which I wrote.

the evening service. On the last Sunday afternoon I was the speaker for their missions rally. The devil was riding on my shoulder and telling me my time there was wasted and I had made no impact on anyone. After the service ended the pianist came to me and said, "I want to give you a big hug. I just love you!" I needed that.

However, at supper that evening a lady sat next to me who tore me apart: "Missionaries have it soft, servants to do their work, they make no sacrifice, they waste their time and are paid for it," and much more. This attitude reminded me that my part is to obey the Lord and seek to please him whether I receive praise or blame from people.

On my last Sunday before departure to return to Burundi, during my private devotions the Lord drew near and I had my own personal "re-commissioning." My promise was Exodus 3:12,14: "Certainly I will be with you. . . I AM has sent you."

That was enough to sustain me all the way.

That day I was at a denomination-wide Missions Celebration in Winona Lake, Indiana. The day concluded with a stirring challenge to commitment by Dr. Charles Kirkpatrick. The Holy Spirit was very near. What a send-off this was for me.

The following Thursday I was on my way back to Burundi. The trip this time was via Montreal where I had to change airports with all my luggage. Keith and Gael Lohnes met me and facilitated the transfer. The Lord took care of all the details of the trip -- about which I'd had a tendency to worry.

Within two weeks of my arrival I unpacked and put away the stuff I brought and all I had packed away. I was given the mission treasury accounts to keep, met in an inter-mission committee meeting, taught Kirundi to Ruth Morris daily, entertained frequent guests for meals, helped Dr. Kuhn get ready to leave for the U. S., saw her and Lois Meredith off at the airport, was busily at work on translation projects with Noah and Joseph, and was starting to train a new literature worker.

My new task was teaching a weekly class in Kirundi at Mweya, an hour's drive from Kibuye. Participants were from the several missions in the area besides our own. I taught the language and also some things about the people and culture of the country. One afternoon I was preparing to teach about the traditional religion of the country (worship of Satan) and some of the occult practices. I began to have very severe blows of pain on the side of my head. I prayed for relief and took some aspirin but it continued intensely. Finally I recognized what it was and said aloud, "Satan, I rebuke you in the name of Jesus, and through his shed blood. Go, and leave me alone." The pain immediately ceased and I was able to continue my work.

Simply Following

23. In All Your Journeying

While on furlough my ophthalmologist warned that I might have a retina detachment in one eye. He described the symptoms that might indicate such an event was happening. Since he had observed the eye carefully during that year, he felt it was safe for me to return to Burundi so long as I understood that if anything happened I must get medical help quickly.

Suddenly one afternoon while I was working, the symptoms described began to appear in that eye. I was advised that in case of a detachment, surgery must be done very soon to save the sight. Our mission doctor, Dr. Marguerite Palmer, advised me to go at once to Nairobi in Kenya, or, if necessary, on to the United States.

For a few days we had been without a car, but Lois Meredith in Bujumbura, on a sudden impulse had decided to come to Kibuye that very afternoon! So the next day, Wednesday, she took me to Bujumbura. First I went to an ophthalmologist, a Russian who knew no English and little

French. He didn't seem very helpful. Next we went to the airline office. There would be no plane to Nairobi until Friday, and there were no available places on it no matter how great my emergency. The next flight would be on Monday. Friday morning I happened to drop my Bible and a poem I slipped in it years before fell out. Here it is:

GO GLADLY
Author Unknown

Child of my love, fear not the unknown morrow,
      Dread not the new demand life makes of thee;
Thy ignorance doth hold no cause for sorrow
      Since what thou knowest not is known to Me.

Stand not in fear thy adversaries counting,
      Dare every peril, save to disobey;
Thou shalt march on, all obstacles surmounting,
      For I, the Strong, will open up the way.

Wherefore go gladly to the task assigned thee,
      Having my promise, needing nothing more
Than just to know, where'er the future find thee,
      In all thy journeying I go before.

That seemed to fit my need exactly. Immediately after reading it, the thought came to me to buy a standby ticket. The airline agent sold it to me but said there was virtually no chance of my getting on that plane. That evening at the proper time Lois and I went to the airport where we found 25 other standbys waiting for the possible six available seats.

We were told to stand with the others. Soon a lady who

worked for the World Health Organization whom Lois had met casually a few days before at a child's birthday party approached us and asked why we were there. Lois explained my situation.

The lady apparently had some clout. She stepped behind the desk and said to the agent, "You have to get this lady on this plane." The agent said it was impossible but finally gave me the last seat. A United Nations representative from another African country got the next-to-last seat. Hearing my problem, he took charge of my luggage (I was told not to lift anything).

Arriving in Nairobi late that evening without a visa or any local currency, I was told by an official to go to a nearby bank to get money changed, then return and buy the visa. At once my seat mate stepped up and handed me enough shillings to buy my visa and a taxi to the city, and would accept no dollars in exchange. Then I phoned the only place I was familiar with, hoping to get a room. They said they had only one available. It had been reserved earlier, but shortly before my call the reservation had been cancelled!

The next day, Saturday, I called the one person in Nairobi that I knew, and she gave me the name of an ophthalmologist. He proved to be a skillful doctor and a Christian! He was also within 36 hours of leaving for a week's safari. I called him and described my symptoms. He said, "Get flat on your back and get someone to bring you to me. I'll probably have to operate tomorrow. It may already be too late."

He spent three hours examining me and explaining the problem. I did not have a retinal detachment, but the vitreous gel of the eye was separating from the retina, leaving a big "floater" right at the macula. There was still danger of a detachment, so I was told to stay in Nairobi for a week until he returned from his trip.

On his return the doctor examined the eye and agreed it was okay for me to return to Burundi so long as I was careful to take certain precautions, for the danger was not over. God was not finished with his miracles, though I already could count at least 10 that were too remarkable to be mere coincidences.

My reservation for the return flight was with Air Zaire, unreliable enough that we sometimes called it "Air Chance." We boarded the plane right on time but then were told we must return inside the terminal for there was a flat tire. We waited seven hours while they flew in another tire from some distance away.

During the luncheon we were served, I sat with three African men, each from a different country. When they asked why I was in Africa and I said I was a missionary, they were filled with questions about being a Christian and how a person can become one. We spent the whole hour talking about Jesus. If they had never heard the way of salvation explained before, they did then.

Later as I sat in the waiting room, a man from India sat next to me and asked the same question: "Why are you in Africa?" Again the discussion was all about Jesus, who he is and how we can know him. I cannot say that any of the four received Christ that day but at least they heard the gospel truths and the Holy Spirit could apply them.

It was good to be back at my work again. No further trouble developed in my eye and gradually the "floater" dissolved. Later on, the right eye developed similar symptoms, but in time that cleared up as well.

A quote from a prayer letter I sent out in February 1979 will give you a general picture of my life at this period:

"On a recent Sunday a team of young people from the Bible school came for our service. They were experiencing revival and bubbling over with joy as they testified and preached about holiness. After the service they went to the hospital to pray with a pastor from Zaire who was here with heart trouble and had been in bed for two or three weeks. He was marvelously healed, got up and began walking around, saying 'Oh, our God is wonderful!' At this very time I was praying at home and God spoke to me so clearly saying, 'I am healing that man.' A couple days later he returned to Zaire eager to tell his people what God had done for him.

"There are also times of hum-drum work -- keeping accounts, or auditing those of others, seeing that the station workers do their job in caring for the grounds, going to committee meetings, typing stencils, and so on. Once in awhile one is tempted to wonder how these activities contribute to bringing people to the Lord, yet they're a necessary part of life. We need your prayers even for these things. The electric system fails or the water system breaks down (as is the case right now), and it's up to me (since we missionaries are all ladies on this station) to get things going again. Not that I know how to do any of that! But I have to try to find someone who does. Thank the Lord, we have a good African assistant.

"Besides these times of excitement, and those of hum-drum-ness, there are other times of just plain harassment from Satan as he attempts to thwart God's work. Equipment breaks down. A band of thieves lives close by and seeks every chance to break in, or at least annoy. Sickness comes. People complain about their salaries. Others fail to do their jobs right. Still others break our hearts by their backsliding or coldness. Attempts are made to bring division into the church.

"But we can say with Paul, 'In all these things we are more than conquerors through him that loved us.' And, 'I have learned in whatsoever state I am therewith to be content.' Thank God for his abiding presence, and the help he gives in every circumstance. He knows the answer to every need."

During this time severe tensions arose in the Burundi church. They were rewriting their Constitution in preparation for becoming a General Conference (which was realized in 1985). Some leaders felt strongly that the mission houses, built by the Department of World Missions (DWM) for missionaries, should be controlled by the national church rather than by the missionaries. They wanted to place national pastors or other leaders in them. Yet the DWM felt this was not acceptable as long as missionaries lived and worked in the country.

After many lengthy discussions, agreement was reached that when missionaries were no longer needed the houses would be the property of the national church. In fact, at the present time as I write, these houses are under the control of the church and nationals are living in many of them.

Another serious problem for the church related to the World Council of Churches (WCC), which had a division for Africa based in Nairobi, Kenya. Our leaders heard of the wonderful financial help this organization provided to member churches. This made a strong appeal to our people for we were always struggling with the limited resources the Free Methodist Church could provide.

The fact that WCC was very liberal doctrinally and supported causes contrary to our beliefs and practices seemed of little importance. The attraction of large amounts of financial support was very strong. Our Director of Missions Dr. Charles Kirkpatrick wired that such action was contrary to the deci-

sions of the General Conference. If taken, the church would
no longer receive FM support.

The Burundi church still voted to go ahead and seek
membership in the WCC. A strong influence in that direction
came from a self-appointed leader of a sister holiness denomination with which we had always worked. I think the whole
question was sort of their declaration of independence from
missionaries. In the other two holiness missions the same
action was agreed upon.

Things went so far that in some places the church took
possession of "mission" cars and houses. It did not go that far
in the Free Methodist Church. However, it was later reported
that some leaders said, "You missionaries lied to us. The
things you said DWM would do if we joined the WCC did not
happen, and we are our own boss now." A few months later
we were told that the leaders never sent in the application for
membership in the WCC. Their purpose had been to push the
North American Free Methodist Church to do more for them.

24. I'd Rather Have Jesus

Serious problems for the church, as well as for the missionaries, lay ahead. A new president had seized the government by a coup. He was definitely anti-Christian and gradually began to curtail church activities.

On June 1, 1979, we first heard rumors that 13 Catholic priests were being expelled from the country by the government, and at least six Protestant missionaries were on the list, four of whom were Free Methodists, whose names were not given. We all sensed the possibility that we might be the ones. No reasons were known for this action.

One evening Faustin, whose conversion is recounted in Chapter 21, came to me and said, "Do you remember you once told me you had a great burden for the youth of our country? Well, God has put that burden on my heart, and I'm going to start a youth group."

My answer was, "Praise the Lord!" I knew he could do far more for them than I could. A few months after my return to the United States I received a letter saying that 60 to 80 youths were participating in Faustin's group.

We began to see and hear little things that made us think the Barundi knew some things we didn't about the future. A man who once asked me to hold securely a sum of money for him came and got it. At Muyebe officials checked all the missionaries' passports, saying, "We need to know more about some of you." Our Kibuye pastor talked with me rather vaguely about some activities in the country.

For me this all came to a head on June 8 when events described on the opening pages of this book took place. Others expelled with me were Warren Land, Nate Thompson, and Lloyd Phillips (VISA). Of course, Della Land and Pris Thompson went along with their husbands though they were not formally named. Dr. Dave and Linda Crandall, recent arrivals at Kibuye, Doris Moore (Meredith) and Ruth Morris did all they could to help Lloyd and me prepare for departure. Eight from the World Gospel Mission also had to leave. In all, about 100 missionaries were expelled, 25 of whom were Protestants. Later we learned that the Kirkpatricks, who were then on furlough, were also included.

On that Sunday afternoon I walked out of the house at Kibuye, my home for 13 years. Most of my personal belongings were in that house including a piano I had purchased two weeks before. I stopped in the doorway and prayed, "Lord, let all these things be used for your work and your glory."

We did not know but what the government would seize it all. Little did I dream that five months later my niece and her husband, Jann and Gary Allen, would move into that house! Eventually much of the furniture and belongings would be brought to me in my new field of labor, while still providing many items for Gary and Jann. How marvelously God takes care of his own.

Our departure was set by the officials for Monday evening. That morning four of our Free Methodist national church leaders came to us in sorrow to share and pray with us. They apologized for their actions toward us in the recent church-mission problems and expressed their love and concern for us. We mingled our tears and prayers and were truly one in the Lord. We all clung to Jesus' words, "I will build my church and the gates of hell shall not prevail against it" (Matt. 16:18).

That afternoon, to our complete surprise, Gerald and Marlene Bates and Jim Stillman arrived from Zaire. Gerald was also area director for our mission. They came with no idea of what was happening. They planned to come days earlier on other business but were delayed until this very day.

What a help and encouragement they were to us. Gerald immediately began to take care of many important details connected with our departure. A host of missionary friends came to see us off and to pray for us.

We heard many different reasons given for our expulsion. One African said it was because Warren and I met with some people from Rwanda in a certain hotel and talked "badly" about Burundi. I had not been in that hotel for over five years. A report in a U. S. newspaper said the Burundi government claimed we were a "threat" to the country and were responsible for some students fleeing. The U. S. State Department told Dr. Charles Kirkpatrick it was because of "interference in the internal affairs of the country."

An Indian man in Bujumbura who was a friend of the missionaries and also of a government official reportedly went to the Burundi immigration office and asked, "What do you mean throwing out these good people along with the bad?"

The reply purportedly was, "We don't want foreigners here who know too much about the country and the language."

Some Africans said it was because of the jealousy of the Catholics. If some priests were expelled they thought some Protestants should be, too. Another African said, "You were chased out by the leaders of the churches. No doubt about it." Later, one of our leaders who worked with me for five years affirmed that our church leaders had nothing to do with choosing which missionaries should leave, but it had been primarily the work of the previously mentioned self-appointed leader of another denomination.

Whatever the given reason, it was a part of the move by the new president to curtail Christian activity. Before long church activity was restricted to Sunday mornings only and that in church buildings. One family was arrested for singing a hymn in their home and another for listening to Christian music on a radio. Stiff restrictions continued until some time much later when there was a change of president.

On arrival in Spring Arbor I felt immediately surrounded by the love and sympathy of our church family, yet inside I felt numb, and the chunk of ice within (mentioned in chapter 1) was still there. Then in mid-week service this hymn, which was new to me, was sung:

In heavenly love abiding,
No change my heart shall fear;
And safe is such confiding,
For nothing changes here.
The storm may roar without me,
My heart may low be laid;
But God is round about me,

And can I be dismayed?

Wherever he may guide me,
No want shall turn me back;
My Shepherd is beside me,
And nothing can I lack.
His wisdom ever waketh
His sight is never dim;
He knows the way he taketh,
And I will walk with him.

Green pastures are before me,
Which yet I have not seen;
Bright skies will soon be o'er me,
Where dark the clouds have been.
My hope I cannot measure,
My path to life is free;
My Savior has my treasure,
And he will walk with me.

by Anna L. Waring

I began to realize that even this devastating experience was within God's plan for me. I could trust him for the outcome. One night after I had gone to bed the whole situation swept over me anew and I wept as I have seldom wept in my adult life. But even the weeping somehow brought cleansing to the grief and pain that had overwhelmed me.

The following Sunday was a beautiful sunny day. I chose to walk to the church which was not far away. As I walked across a small field beside the church I felt totally surrounded and wrapped by God's love. All the beauty of nature and the sunshine itself were God's love holding me close. In that moment I knew I would rather have Jesus and have every-

thing just like it was:
- stripped of the work I loved,
- stripped of the friends whom I might never see again,
- stripped of nearly everything I owned,

than to have everything the world could give me but without Jesus. The glow and warmth of that revelation stayed with me for a long time. Even today when I think of that experience my eyes fill with tears of joy at this marvelous expression of Jesus' love and presence.

A few days later a letter arrived from an English missionary in Burundi. This very dear friend said, "God never takes anything away without giving something *better* in its place." How true that has proven in my life. Soon after, the Kirkpatrick children gave me a poster that read, "What seems to be the end may be just a new beginning." That was indeed prophetic of God's leading for me.

My pain and sorrow were eased somewhat by the presence in Spring Arbor of Jim and Martha Kirkpatrick and their children who were then on furlough. We had worked together in Burundi since 1964 and they were dear to me. Of all the people in Spring Arbor the Kirkpatricks could best understand the situation and empathize. In fact, their future was affected as well as mine.

Kirkpatricks and I were invited to Winona Lake to consult with our mission executives. They expressed confidence in us and shared their concern for the Burundi church. Possibilities for our future work were discussed, but it was too early to make any definite decisions.

My preference, if it was not possible to return to Burundi, was to go to Rwanda, a country very similar to Burundi in culture and language. I already was acquainted with some of the church leaders there. Of course, it remained to be seen whether the Rwanda church would even want me. Many uncertainties still lay ahead, and my nature is to like to have each step clearly laid out before me.

The next few months for me were a time of learning to trust and wait for God's plan and timing. Sometimes I felt as if there was no place for me. I even had a hard time finding an apartment to live in but was graciously cared for in the home of Harold and Sally Trevan while I searched. At every furlough they have helped me so much. In due time I found an apartment. After three months in it, a couple who lived in Arbor View Estates offered me the use of their apartment rent-free while they were in Florida.

Before long the Rwanda church let the DWM know that they welcomed me to Rwanda, primarily to translate the *Free Methodist Book of Discipline* into the Kinyarwanda language. This made me feel good but it took some time for all the details to be worked out until I could be given a definitive appointment.

In August a meeting of the Free Methodist World Fellowship was held in Winona Lake with representatives coming from most of our missions. Three nationals would be there from Burundi. I wondered how they felt about me and how they would treat me. I was invited to be there for the opening service on Sunday to interpret for Rev. Matayo, a district superintendent in Burundi, who would preach. So I was in the hotel lobby late Saturday night when the men arrived from their plane trip.

I need not have wondered. All three of them ran up and gave me a big hug, which in their culture was perfectly all right. Genuine warmth and caring were expressed in that spontaneous gesture. Rev. Aaron Ruhumuriza and his wife, Edith, then leader of the Rwanda Free Methodist Church, were with the group. They too evidenced their love and appreciation for me. This was healing balm to my pain of spirit.

On Sunday morning Rev. Aaron, who knows English well, spoke at the 8:45 service. His message seemed to be especially for me -- even others remarked on that. Then Rev. Matayo preached at the next service with me interpreting, and I sensed the Holy Spirit's help. Throughout the day at different events and situations, I was called on to interpret for the delegates and translate some written reports. This work made me feel that I was still part of the Burundi church. One committee requested Rev. Matayo to ask me to continue doing translation work for them while here in the United States. I was delighted to do it even though I wouldn't have a national at my side to assist me. The material would be edited by nationals in Burundi when they received it from me.

The World Convocation and General Conference of the Free Methodist Church began a few days later in Indianapolis. I was invited to attend which was a rare privilege. Usually I was not in the United States for these special events. Lois Meredith and I shared a room in the home of a church member.

How we enjoyed being together! Having just arrived recently from Burundi, she was able to bring me up to date on events there since my departure. The church was indeed undergoing a time of pressure and persecution. Throughout the whole week I did private interpretation for the delegates in little groups within the audience, even going to committees with them. Keeping up constantly with what was said was difficult but I was grateful for the opportunity to serve in this way.

While there it was wonderful to meet many friends from across the years. Of course, there were those whose names I could not recall who remembered me from my deputation ministry in previous years. I was frequently asked questions about my expulsion from Burundi, and my future plans. Regarding the latter I hadn't much to say, for no decision had yet been reached. Bob Cranston and John Schlosser, missionaries in the Philippines, begged me to consider going there. They said I was greatly needed. I could only tell them my future was in the hands of God and the Missionary Board.

Following General Conference the delegates remained in the United States for a few more days and visited in various churches. Aaron, Edith, and Noah came to Spring Arbor and spoke in the mid-week service. I had the privilege of having Noah in my home for lunch one day and Aaron and Edith the next day. They were able to talk freely about conditions in their respective countries.

Noah filled me in on some details regarding our expulsion that I hadn't known. Aaron and Edith told me a little of their past history which was fascinating. God has led them in miraculous ways. I was particularly interested in Aaron's account of a time early in his ministry when he was desperately ill with tuberculosis in Kibogora Hospital. People prayed for him and doctors did all they could but he only grew worse.

One day a group came to his room to really lay hold of God for him. Aaron said, "During that prayer time I totally committed myself to God. I told him I wanted him to have all my strength and energy and to use me to the highest and fullest of my capabilities." He felt within himself that he was healed and the next time x-rays were taken his lungs were completely clear.

Aaron has sought to keep that commitment across the years. He said, "Sometimes now I feel overwhelmed with my responsibilities and tasks. Then Edith reminds me that God is just doing what I asked him to do long ago in that hospital room."

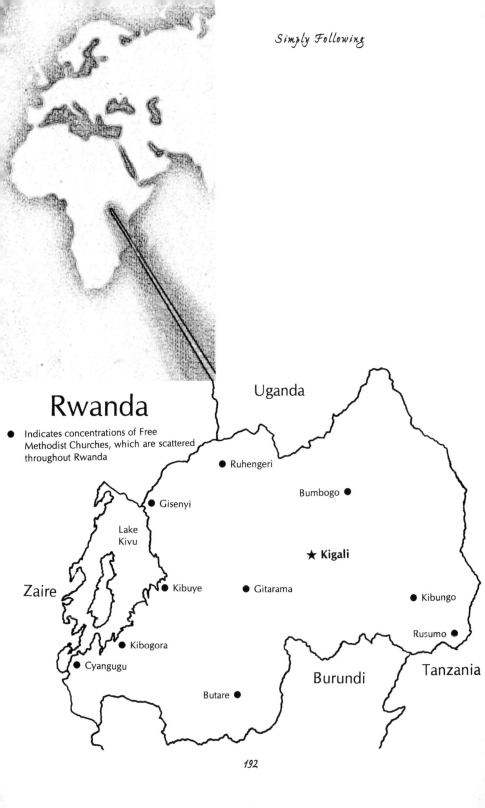

Rwanda

● Indicates concentrations of Free
Methodist Churches, which are scattered
throughout Rwanda

Uganda

● Ruhengeri

Bumbogo ●

● Gisenyi

Lake
Kivu

★ **Kigali**

Zaire

● Kibuye   ● Gitarama

● Kibungo

Rusumo ●

● Kibogora

● Cyangugu

Burundi

Tanzania

Butare ●

25. Transition

The Missions Department did not take long to set up a deputation schedule for me. Many of my free days I spent planning messages, or putting together slide sets with commentary. Soon after my arrival various nearby churches invited me to speak. Not many missionaries get expelled from their adoptive countries so people were curious about the whole experience. Some (including even a few at our church headquarters at first) thought we surely must have done something terrible. But as the whole picture of the oppression of the churches there became clearer, people began to understand. Other missions in Burundi were beginning to "nationalize" and missionaries were being withdrawn.

By September a full schedule of meetings was underway including a two-week tour in Kansas. At one church after a potluck meal the people went into the sanctuary. The meeting was opened by the pastor saying (and I quote verbatim): "I don't know anything about her nor what she wants to do, so I'll just turn the service over to her." No song, no prayer, no mention of my name or work! This concise introduction sort of floored me for a moment. But the Lord met with us and we had a good service anyway.

Christmas that year was spent with my friend Genevieve Strayer in California. We met while I worked among the Japanese in Stockton, California, lived together four years, and thought a great deal of one another. That Christmas was saddened by the death of her nephew, Andy, an alcoholic who was picked up unconscious and taken to a hospital where he died.

One morning early in January while I was in the bathtub the Lord dropped down a huge blessing on me. A bit later as I was reading in the Word he made Exodus 23:20 very real to me: "Behold I send an angel before thee to keep thee in the way, and to bring thee to the place which I have prepared." In due time that promise was richly fulfilled. After a couple more weeks with Genevieve, I resumed my deputation ministry in California, making new friends and meeting quite a few whom I already knew.

Back home by February, I was soon making preparations for going to Rwanda, even while continuing my visits to churches. Speaking at the church in Greenville, Illinois, was pretty scary, this being a college church, yet the Lord enabled me to minister there and people responded.

Soon the packing process was begun, sorting out which things to take and what to leave here. Not until 10 days before my departure date were all my documents in order.

In March my ophthalmologist found holes in my retinas and sealed them with nitrous oxide. It took a few days for my eyes to get back to normal, but the healing process was soon complete. Packing my barrels for shipping one day, it was so hot that I perspired freely. The next day there were two inches of snow on the ground! That's Michigan!

My last Sunday in Spring Arbor, Pastor Hendricks prayed a "commissioning" prayer for me at the altar and anointed me with oil. It meant a lot to me that Canja, a student from Burundi, joined others praying around me -- an African praying for me as I went to Africa.

On April 25, 1980, with a good group of Spring Arbor friends to see me off, I set my face toward Africa again, not sure what awaited me there, but very sure of the one who was leading me. Two days later I was in Rwanda and the next day reached Kibogora where I would spend six years.

I was overwhelmed by the amazing beauty of the mountains towering above Lake Kivu, with four volcanoes ranged along the horizon (see cover photo). Many times I stood on my front porch, looked at the magnificent scene before me, and praised God for the privilege of serving him in such a setting.

Within a couple days of my arrival, Louise Snyder placed in my hands the records and accounts of Literature and of Child Care -- to be turned over later to Esther Knoll (Teal).

A concentrated study was soon under way to learn the many differences between Kirundi and Kinyarwanda. A month later the Snyders were on their way to the United States for furlough. I was on my own.

Kibogora is not a town or city, just a hill made into a mission station with church, hospital, elementary school, secondary level school, literature center, and numerous residences. At that time 16 adult missionaries and seven children were living there. At first I lived in a large house with Evelyn Rupert (Heath) and Virginia Strait, but when school was out for the summer some of the missionaries (including Evelyn) returned to the United States, and single occupancy homes became available. My home from then on was half of a duplex with a nice view of the lake. Soon Mim and Irvin Cobb and their three sons returned to the house where we had been living. How my life has been enriched by fellow missionaries I have worked with across the years!

Before long we had organized a translation team and were ready to tackle the *Free Methodist Book of Discipline.* Pastor Epayineto Rwamunyana, the first Free Methodist Christian in Rwanda and a real man of God, agreed to help with this important work. His help made me very happy. Working with him was fun. He was so thrilled to be getting this book they had longed for for many years. Occasionally our work was interrupted by: "Praise the Lord! I'm so glad our church believes that!" or something similar. Many were the joys we shared in that fashion as the work progressed. Pastor Aaron Ruhumuriza also met with us when he could. He said that as he read what we translated he got so blessed he forgot to check for errors or possible changes.

Oh yes! I was also asked to teach 10 hours a week in the Bible school. This six-year program trained students to be pastors, lay ministers, or elementary school teachers. At first this teaching was frustrating because I wanted to get on with the translating. Gradually though, I found that teaching was a real opportunity for ministry and I was blessed by the contacts with the youth of the church.

In a Personal Evangelism class for which I felt poorly qualified, I asked the students to write an essay telling how they had been brought to Christ. The papers were to be unsigned. Through this I found that in a class of about 30 students, six acknowledged that they had never accepted Christ as their Savior. I was appalled that they could be in that type of school for almost six years without making this important choice. I spoke to the class briefly about this and then said, "If there's anyone in class who would like someone to pray with you, please let me know."

As I walked out of the class, Andrew practically ran after me. "When can we meet together to pray?" he asked. We could not find a time when we were both free until the next morning. Andrew came to my home that next day. I was sure from one look at his face that something BIG had happened. He blurted out, "Yesterday when I left you, my sins were so heavy I just couldn't wait until today. So I went to my room, knelt by my bed and asked Jesus to forgive my sins. And he did!" Of that I had no doubt. We began to share some scripture verses and to thank Jesus for what he did in Andrew's life.

Now let's fast forward for a little bit. In Rwanda when students receive a teaching certificate, the government assigns them to the place where they are to teach. The next fall found Andrew teaching in an elementary school quite some distance away from Kibogora. Soon a letter from him reached me.

"Nearly all the other teachers here claim to be atheists," he wrote.

My reply read, "Maybe that's why God placed you there."

A few weeks later, another letter from Andrew: "We now have a Bible study for teachers during the noon hour. Most of the other teachers are attending and they're calling me *Pastor.*"

From that time on Andrew began to visit in the homes of his students and others, sharing with the families the good news about Jesus. He became active in the Free Methodist church nearby. Now after three years as a refugee -- and a godly leader in a camp -- he is back in that same community.

Let's go back now to those beginning days in Rwanda. I'm

sure the prayers for me by many friends enabled me to adjust quickly to this new situation.

It took time to know the church people and for them to know me. Once when we three ladies were still living together a young woman who worked in our home related to me some problems she was experiencing at home. I said, "Let's pray

Andrew in 1996 leading a choir of the church he worked with in a refugee camp.

about it now." We prayed for perhaps five minutes, then went back to our work. For years after whenever Marita saw me, she would say, "I remember the time you prayed that God's will be done in me. God answered your prayer."

Praying for another often requires putting feet to our prayers. At one point I began to think about Aroni, our head workman. He is a very capable mechanic, chauffeur, plumber, and maintenance man. He can fix almost anything, but as I thought about him I realized I had not heard him give a testimony. I wondered if he was saved.

I began to pray for him, especially asking God to send someone to talk to him about his spiritual condition. I seldom had occasion to talk with him, but one day on my way home from work I passed by the shop and exchanged a few words of greeting with him. As I went on my way, again I prayed, "Oh Lord, please send someone to talk with Aroni."

At once the Lord said, "What about you?"

I replied, "Lord, if I'm the one, you'll have to send him to me and give me an opening."

Less than an hour later there was a knock on my door! Who but Aroni? He rarely came to my house! When he had finished his business, I almost let him go, but the Lord said, "I brought him to you. Aren't you going to do anything about it?"

So I said, "Aroni, may I ask you a personal question?" He smilingly agreed so I asked, "How are you getting along spiritually? I've had a burden to pray for you for a long time."

He dropped his head, saying, "Oh! Thank you for praying for me! I'm not getting along at all well. I've been doing things I know I shouldn't. Please keep on praying for me."

A month or so later Aroni stood up in a special service, publicly confessed his sins, and accepted Jesus as his Savior. What joy flooded my heart as I could see that God had allowed me to have a little part in this important decision.

God was also teaching his people about the joys of tithing. In the annual conference one year a lengthy discussion had gone on regarding the budget, particularly in reference to the salaries of four men to be sent to new areas and who should each be paid 6,000 francs a month. No solution was found, and the spirit in the talking was deteriorating.

Then the conference superintendent got up and said, "I

haven't been paid my salary for seven months but the Lord has met all my needs. He'll do the same for these young men. I started out at 20 francs per month and I never went hungry." They began to sing their praise chorus, "May Jesus be praised."

Then a pastor who was also a carpenter got up and put 1,000 francs on the table and said, "This is for those new areas, and I have faith that God will multiply it a hundred times."

Another jumped up and joyfully put down 500 francs. Soon they were spiritedly singing "Bringing in the sheaves" and placing money on the table. In about 10 minutes 28,000 francs ($280) had been given. Talk about hilarious giving! That was it!

In a pastors' retreat a new area was presented to us as a place where the church needed to move in. A Swiss economist visiting this place, known as Bumbogo, was impressed by the excessive drinking and low moral standards. He reported to the government that a Free Methodist Church was needed there. When asked why that particular church, he said it was the only group he knew about that worked to prevent drunkenness.

This story was related to our church leaders and they felt this was an open door we should enter. So now this question was presented to the pastors' retreat. Should we enter? Would anyone volunteer for this new and difficult situation?

The next morning Elizaphan, a lay minister, recounted how God talked to him during the night about Bumbogo. If the church would send him, and if his wife agreed, he was willing to move to Bumbogo to take the gospel there. Later his wife agreed.

Pastor Aaron Ruhumuriza was the church leader. He lost

no time going to visit the area along with some other pastors. Arrangements were made to purchase property there with a good house on it that could be both a residence and a place of worship. But a few weeks later when Pastor Aaron went to Bumbogo along with Elizaphan and his wife, he found the owner of the property was still living in the nice house which his wife was unwilling to relinquish. In its stead he offered a poor little house, at the same time promising that in due time they would get the larger house.

Elizaphan circulated word that the first Sunday service would be held on the hillside, but no one came. Not discouraged, Elizaphan and his wife went into their little house and recommitted themselves to God and to Bumbogo.

When Pastor Aaron presented Elizaphan to the local mayor, the mayor was not impressed, but Rev. Aaron asked him to give Elizaphan a trial of three months before making a decision. When Aaron returned after three months the mayor said, "Don't you dare take that man away from us. He's the best thing that has happened to this place."

The work at Bumbogo grew dramatically. Before the 1994 war there were 11 little churches on the surrounding hills. Today after a sojourn as a refugee, Elizaphan is back in Rwanda, still leading people to Jesus.

Paganism, or the traditional religion of the country known as animism, still holds many people in its grip -- about 10% of the population when the last figures were compiled. This traditional religion teaches that spirits, both good and evil, inhabit many objects such as rocks and trees.

Pastor Marc had recently been sent to a place where there was a "fetish" tree which supposedly had certain powers, such as for healing. People offered sacrifices and prayers to this tree which was on the property of a new Christian who in his zeal wanted the tree cut down.

Pastor Marc with a group of new Christians went to carry out the man's wishes. However, word soon spread and a mob of devotees of the tree came. Many of them were wild from taking a drug. They grabbed Marc and beat him fiercely, ripped his clothes, and took his shoes. Before long a local merchant who knew Marc came by in his truck and rescued Marc from his attackers. Marc says that now he understands a little more of Jesus' sufferings.

The latest report I've heard is that the tree still stands but is no longer worshipped. A long-standing court case prevented the owner of the property from cutting it down. However, within eight months of Pastor Marc's experience, eight of those who attacked him died of accidents or sudden illness. The remaining ones went to Pastor Marc begging him to pray that their lives would be spared.

* * * * * * * *

It was a treat for me to have the Kirkpatricks living in the other half of my duplex. We had been good friends for a long time. Sometimes I was inclined to feel a little envious of Martha, for the Rwandese women often came to see her and she gave them much spiritual help.

But I was usually either at my typewriter or mimeograph machine. One day while working with the mimeo, I began talking with the Lord. "Lord, shouldn't I be out visiting the women in their homes, or finding young people to talk to about you?"

It seemed that the Lord answered me, "My child, are you doing the work I gave you to do?"

Thoughtfully I replied, "Yes, Lord, I am doing it the best I

Simply Following

know how."

So tenderly came his answer, "That's all I ask of you." His peace and joy flooded my heart anew.

Translation of the *Free Methodist Book of Discipline* was finally completed with much rejoicing. The 180 stencils required were all typed and ready to make copies but for some unknown reason the mimeo machine was spilling water out with the ink and making the pages a mess. Where did the water come from? I tried three different brands of ink. Same result!

In the midst of this a letter came from Pastor Aaron, who now lived in Kigali, saying that he must have five copies of the complete book within a week to present to government officials. And my machine was running water! I had already checked through the entire machine and found no reason for the problem, but once more I went through it without result.

At last in desperation I placed my hands on the machine and prayed, "Lord, please heal the machine or show me what to do." I tried one small procedure which I had done previously, put a stencil on the machine, and began running off beautiful, clean pages! Praise the Lord! Across several years and hundreds of stencils since then, the machine never spilled water again!

Some time later Pastor Aaron thanked me for my work on the *Discipline*. He said, "I'm sure it was God who brought you here at this time. It's not just that he turned the worst -- your expulsion from Burundi -- into the best. Rather, he brought about the best through the worst."

A fairly frequent feature of life at Kibogora was the necessary trips to Kigali, the capital, to do government business, for special meetings, or to shop. At any time the roads were horrendous (they have since been paved). In rainy season we never knew what a trip might include. A conference-wide women's meeting was scheduled for Kigali in November when the rains were copious. I was to be the speaker.

At best, a trip might take seven hours, but at worst -- well, anything! Elaine Williamson, a good mechanic and courageous driver, Anna, a VISA nurse, and I, with several Rwandese women set out early one morning for the Kigali meeting.

All went well for three hours. Then suddenly before us was a huge mudhole. There had been a landslide, and a truck was caught in the middle of it. We waited for three hours while about 40 workers dug the truck out with hoes and shovels. Immediately the workers shoved logs back in the hole so we couldn't go through until we agreed to pay 1,000 francs (about $10). Even then, it took awhile to pay the money to the right guy and then gently move ahead, pushing men out of the way while some tried to slash our tires.

At last we thought we were through, but alas! A mile farther on we came to another landslide! But this time the men were pleasant and worked with a will. We paid them and were soon on our way. Needless to say, our seven-hour trip took 12 hours.

The local women went ahead with the first meeting at which 30 women went forward to pray, many for the first time ever. So God didn't need *us* to get things going! The meetings went on through Sunday with a gracious outpouring of God's Spirit. One of the new converts, a harlot originally from Kibogora, really got right with God and continued on with him, as did many other women.

Kanyandekwe and Elena were neighbors of our church at Kibogora. Back in the 1970s he led a movement to legalize the use of alcoholic beverages in Free Methodist churches. When that failed, he and many of his friends withdrew from the church and have opposed it ever since. Being a government school inspector, he thought he needed to drink wherever he went for inspection.

Elena, participating in a women's Bible study group, recognized her own need of a real relationship with Christ and made genuine commitments. One commitment was to be a better wife and more loving to her husband, which she endeavored to do, but his heart remained hard and unyielding. During the 1994 war, Kanyandekwe and Elena fled as refugees. On their return in 1997 he was imprisoned. There he became very ill and was taken to the hospital. Soon he asked for a Bible and after a time was wonderfully saved. Then his health improved and he was returned to the prison where he gives a beautiful testimony.

My ophthalmologist in Michigan told me I must be sure to have my eyes examined annually. I flew to Nairobi (700 miles away) for this examination. To my surprise, again there were several holes in each retina. Having been warned about how to be careful, I was told to return in six months. In a prayer letter soon after I asked for prayer for my eyes. My dear friend Mary Loretta Rose once more accepted some responsibility for this and was anointed by proxy for my eyes. On my return to Nairobi six months later, the doctor found that the holes had sealed themselves! Rather, God had sealed them in answer to believing prayer.

A frequent visitor in my home was Japhet. Sometimes he was sober and sometimes drunk. Japhet was an alcoholic. He had formerly been a capable nurse at the hospital but alcohol was destroying him. Once he wrote me a letter which I quote: "I want to thank you for the zeal you always have to pray for me. I remember the time you asked me why I didn't stop drinking. Not having a suitable answer, I told you, 'Those who drink will go to heaven, too.' I went home that day feeling I had completely broken off our friendship, but you said, 'We'll keep on praying for you.' I didn't believe you would because I was blind in matters of salvation. But the other day you wrote to say, 'I am still praying for you.' I knew then that you are a real Christian, because you love even people who refuse to get saved. From that day on I've begun to change. The other day I received Jesus Christ as my Savior."

I wish I could say that Japhet continued walking with Jesus. The next 10 years he was up and down, periodically repenting and serving the Lord for two or three months, then slipping back into his old ways. But when I visited Rwanda in

When I visited Rwanda in 1993 I saw Japhet and his wife. He and most of his family were killed in the slaughter that took place about seven months after my visit.

1993, Japhet's face showed the peace and joy he had found. About seven months after that, he and most of his family were killed in the awful slaughter that took place. I trust he made it to heaven.

26. Still Following

Normally our terms of service are four years followed by a year of home leave. I knew by 1986 I would need to retire. Yet a six-year term seemed rather long, so I decided to come to the United States in 1984 for six weeks at my own expense. I chose to come in the spring because I love to experience the new awakening life of that time of year.

That was also the year of my 50th anniversary of our high school graduation in Spring Arbor -- a bonus I had not thought of when I made my plans. What a pleasure it was on that occasion to see friends whom I had not met for many years, some in fact, not since the 1934 graduation. Some of the contacts made then have continued by correspondence until the present.

Various reunions with family members and others occurred during those six weeks. I stayed with Trevans, and Sally graciously entertained my many visiting friends. The Kirkpatricks were having their furlough in Spring Arbor so we were frequently together. I was asked to speak a few times, but not enough that it was a heavy burden. So this six-week interlude was a time to recharge my batteries, hear good messages in my native tongue, and renew old friendships.

Soon enough the fun and games were over and I was back at work again, delighted with the privilege of serving the Lord at Kibogora. Plenty of translation projects awaited me. And I had a new girl working for me. As usual, patience was greatly needed in that process. Once I found two broken glasses on the shelf with the good ones. "How did these get broken?" I inquired.

Reply, "I don't know. I guess they just broke themselves sitting there on the shelf." I soon learned that no matter what the catastrophe, she could never say, "I did it. I'm sorry."

At last I asked her why she couldn't take responsibility for burnt food, broken dishes, damaged clothes in the laundry, or whatever. She replied, "Why should I say I'm sorry when I'll probably do it again soon?"

Why, indeed! "Patience, Lord, give me patience -- NOW!" I stopped to remember that these were all new things, gadgets, and experiences she hadn't encountered in her own lifestyle and sympathy for her crept into my heart.

* * * * * * * *

One day after a church service, a little, rather shrivelled lady came to me to ask, "Would you have something you could give me to carry water in?"

"Oh, I think I can find something. Come to my house." I had seen her at church and heard her testify that Jesus saved her. At home I found a gallon jug I'd bought soap in.

She thanked me profusely and added, "I have no family at all and no place to sleep at night. But I love Jesus! And some day I'm going to live with him! Oh! I love Jesus!" Again thanking me warmly, she went on her way.

I went back into my house and wept. A great need like that and I gave her a jug of little value to me but precious to her. Water often had to be carried for some distance. Soon I asked the pastor about her.

"Yes," he told me, "her story is true. Her husband died several years ago. They had no children so his family made her leave their home. Ever since then she has wandered around and stayed with whoever will take her in for a night, a week, or a year."

Yet she was often in church. I asked the pastor if the church could give her a little plot of ground where she could grow some beans and make a little house. I would provide the roof (usually the costly part of building a house). He accepted that responsibility, and soon she had her own little place. How she praised God!

* * * * * * * *

Communication sometimes isn't easy, yet it is so important to the transmission of the gospel. A deaf-mute man was given the gospel sufficiently to receive Christ. He indicated that he wanted to be baptized. When the pastor endeavored to find out how he knew he was saved the deaf man went and got a lantern with a dirty chimney. He pointed to the lantern, then to his heart. Then he carefully cleaned the chimney and lit the lantern. He pointed up, then to himself and began to laugh heartily with real joy. Could you express your testimony that well, without words?

* * * * * * * *

In 1985 the Free Methodist Church in Rwanda, with
approval of the General Conference of North America,
became a full general conference. Bishop Clyde Van Valin had
come from the U. S. to preside at the first sitting of this new
general conference where Rev. Aaron Ruhumuriza was formally elected as Rwanda's first Free Methodist bishop. He had
long been the main leader of the church. It was my privilege
to interpret for Bishop Van Valin so I had a small part in this
momentous event. On Saturday morning of that week the big
stadium in Kigali was the site for the public consecration of
Bishop Aaron.

Many dignitaries were present: the President of Rwanda
with other government officials, our Free Methodist General
Missionary Secretary Elmore Clyde, other guests from the
United States, bishops of other denominations and other
nations (such as Uganda and Kenya), plus a great many Free
Methodist members and many friends of the church.

Bishop Aaron Ruhumuriza's message, after he was conse-
crated by Bishop Van Valin, focused on his being sent by God
to be a shepherd. Here are a few brief quotes from his message:

"As long as God keeps me in this work, I want to answer
his voice as did Isaiah the prophet when he said, 'Here am I,
send me' (Is. 6:8). I hear myself saying, 'I'm coming, God, send
me.' I'm coming to be sent as a shepherd, whether in sun or
rain, day or night, near or far, to the great and the small. I
know I am weak, but I am used by the power of God. 'I can do
all things through Christ who strengthens me' (Philippians
4:13). I am not terribly brave, but I serve the one who gives
courage to those who obey him. Most of all, I am willing to be
sent, depending on the power of Almighty God, for I know

that without the Spirit of God I am nothing at all, so I trust only in the power of the one who sends me."

As 1986 was rapidly drawing closer, I began to worry and fret about details of my return to America. I decided to go in April, I guess because I love spring. But April is the month of our heaviest rains in Rwanda. I would have extra baggage because of leaving for good, so how would I handle that? And, though I had my name on the list for an apartment in the retirement center in Spring Arbor, what would I do if there was none available?

To add to these concerns, some pastors kept telling me I couldn't be spared and I didn't really *have* to retire right away. Why should I leave when I was needed and didn't appear to be ill? One day while I was mimeographing, the Lord said to me so clearly, "Stop your worrying. I'm going to take care of it all." Here is how he kept his promise:

About 10 days before my departure from Kibogora, I knew a routine meeting of the Executive Committee of the Central

Some of the books we translated and published in Rwanda.

Africa Area Fellowship was to occur there, but I was totally unprepared for the main event of that weekend -- a farewell for me. There were six or eight Burundi pastors, including Bishop Noah, several from Zaire, and many, of course, from Rwanda.

Martha Kirkpatrick was the organizer and planner of this beautiful occasion, though I'm sure others assisted. I feel so unworthy of all the wonderful things that were said, the love that was expressed by words and gifts. What precious memories of that day will remain with me always! I'd like to include here Bishop Aaron's remarks on that occasion:

"We are very happy to have the opportunity to thank you for all the years you have given yourself to serve in Rwanda and Burundi. You have worked in Africa for 42 years of your life. We count it an offering you have given to your Lord Jesus Christ, and as a gift you have given to the church of Christ wherever you have worked. We'll try to say in a few words some of the things you have done during the scant six years you have been in Rwanda:

- You have trained many children and done it well. Now they are grown men and women.

- You have written many books which are useful to people.

- You assisted in the translation of the *Book of Discipline* and are still working on it, so now the Church will not be working in confusion but has a pattern to follow.

- In all the work you have done we know that you worked zealously, obeying the command in Mark 12:30, 'Therefore love the Lord your God with all your heart and all your soul and all your mind and all your strength.'

- Frequently, in all the committees you were in, you expressed your opinions, without keeping them to yourself, and they were valuable.

- Because of your zeal and faithfulness, the people have given you a Kinyarwanda name, which I've decided to tell you, even though you didn't know it. They have baptized you 'Miss Zeal.'

"Most of those who have followed your life, have noted another special characteristic you have, which not many have. They say that you have never once tried to change someone's opinion, whoever it may be, without first allowing him to explain it. For that you deserve to be praised.

"Dear Miss Zeal, the Free Methodist Church in Rwanda and also in Burundi has had the gift of your presence for a long time, for which we praise God. Dear Miss Zeal, you have been a good example to many in your speech, your actions, your work, and we pray that God will reward you for this.

"Our dear friend whom we love, Miss Betty Ellen Cox, Miss Zeal, it is true you are about to leave Rwanda but you have not left our hearts. We will continue to pray for you, as you will for us. God Almighty is the one who will recompense you for the sacrifice, dignity, and faithfulness which you have shown throughout your life, though we could not possibly find a worthy gift to give you.

"May the Lord continue to be with you until that time when we shall meet again in the heavenly Kingdom where there will be no more sadness nor parting. In the name of the Free Methodist Church in Rwanda, *Bishop Aaron Ruhumuriza.*"

The plaque that was given me that day hangs now in my living room, bearing these words:

The Rwanda and Burundi
Free Methodist Conferences
Present this plaque to

Miss Betty Ellen Cox
in recognition of her 42 years (1944-1986)
of diligent, dedicated and faithful service
of mind, spirit and strength
in the building of God's kingdom among us.
We love, respect, and cherish you.
Bishop Ruhumuriza Aaron - Rwanda
Bishop Nzeyimana Noé - Burundi

The conclusion of this wonderful occasion was when the two bishops placed their hands on me and commissioned me as their missionary to America while the other pastors stood with their hands outstretched toward me. I take this commission very seriously and feel I am still a part of the Church in Rwanda and Burundi, as well as of the U. S. church.

Sales to missionaries, sales to Africans, give-aways to both, packing what remained in suitcases and footlockers, instructions to my successors, and tearful farewells -- all this was the wind down to 42 years of simply following Jesus in Africa, step by step and day by day.

The Lord really kept his hand on that trip to the United States. The day the Cobbs took me to Kigali was mostly sunny and pleasant -- no mud-holes to cross! I shipped three footlockers by air which reached the U. S. about a week after I did. My luggage with me was three pieces, on which I expected to pay excess baggage for the third one. But this confused the officials, so they let it go for $100.

Vern DeMille's mother, who had been visiting them, was flying with me to Brussels on her way to Canada. When I reached Detroit about 3:30 p.m., just 27 hours after leaving Kigali, the Trevans, Whitemans, and Lloyd Phillips were waiting for me. In all my travels I never went through arrival procedures as quickly as I did that day.

My remaining concern was to acquire an apartment. I was shown a second-floor apartment at Arbor View Estates, but by the time they were ready for me to move in, just two and a half weeks after my arrival, I was suddenly offered a first floor one. Surely this had been in God's plan all along.

My first two years in the United States were spent in full time home ministry. What a blessing it was to have a first floor apartment and not to have to carry my bulky luggage up and down the stairs week in and week out.

I can say with Joshua: "You know with all your heart and soul that not one of all the good promises the Lord your God gave you has failed. Every promise has been fulfilled" (Joshua 23:14). Such joy! Just to let him promise and lead, while I simply obey and follow.

27. Epilogue

Retirement is rather fun, at least in some ways. You are free to choose how to use your time. Naturally, I opted to continue translation work as far as possible. I was invited to represent our church in an interdenominational (holiness churches) "French Task Force" (later called Mission Literature Association). The goal was to produce holiness literature in French. It wasn't surprising that I was soon translating, writing, or editing books in French.

Then our Burundi Church called on me for some help with an updated *Book of Discipline* in Kirundi, and of course, there were on-going projects in Kinyarwanda. I have loved every bit of it, except perhaps a few times when I had to work against a deadline, as in, "Please have this done by such and such a date."

At least two lovely surprises have come my way:

1) In 1988 both of my Alma Maters chose to honor me. Spring Arbor College made me an honorary Doctor of Literature. Greenville College named me an Alumnus of the

As part of the "French Task Force," it's not surprising that in retirement I was soon developing holiness literature in French.

Year. It took a little juggling and the assistance of some friends for me to be in Greenville Saturday evening and in Spring Arbor Sunday afternoon, but both honors were received with joy and thanks to God. Also, I had the privilege at another time of seeing Bishops Aaron and Noah receive honorary doctorates at Greenville College.

2) The second surprise was the receipt of one large gift and several smaller ones which enabled me to go back to Rwanda for two months in 1993. Isn't the Lord good to his children? What a privilege this was. I saw many old friends in different places, met new workers in the churches, and taught young people!

Harriet Bolodar and I travelled together going out, and she has stayed there until now. We were there in time for the annual missionary retreat at Kumbya. Such a blessing this was! Many friends of years gone by were there as well as new young families. The Holy Spirit truly met with us. This was also one of the last times the Kumbya facility was used, for during the 1994 war most of the buildings were destroyed and the contents taken.

From Kumbya, Melli (Andrews) Johnson and I went to Butare where the Kirkpatricks lived to begin a four-week course in English for about 40 seminary students. This was quite an experience. We lived in the home of a professor at the seminary who was in Europe for the summer. Closets were all locked so we lived out of our suitcases. Electricity was off

Spring Arbor College awarded me the honorary Doctor of Literature degree in 1988.

Melli Johnson, our cook Laetitia, and I
at Butare, September 1993.

more than on and the stove and all lights were electric. But
Martha provided us with a one-burner bottled gas plate and a
gas lamp, so we managed.

The experience was fascinating. Some of the students
were a real blessing to us and I hope we were to them. From
there I went back to Kibogora for a very happy two weeks of
meeting with old friends. How could I have guessed that within seven months many of these would be in heaven with the
Lord? How often I have thanked the Lord for that time in
Rwanda so shortly before the ravages of 1994 took place.

Across these retirement years my main interests have
been just two: providing literature for the central Africa countries and being active in the Spring Arbor Free Methodist
Church. In 1989 I attended the General Conference of our
church in Seattle and again in 1995 in Anderson, Indiana.

My heart aches as reports continue to come of the losses
in our central Africa countries, of the sufferings of our people

in refugee camps, and of those who have been bereaved. Probably one million people have died in Rwanda plus many hundreds of thousands in both Burundi and Zaire (now the Democratic Republic of Congo), and the end is not yet.

In spite of these troubles, my faith is bright with confidence that God has not forsaken his people. He will yet build his church for his own glory. Indeed, reports of revival are coming in. Already in 1998 we hear news that church membership in Rwanda now approaches 90,000!

So the road leads on. I continue to simply follow the Lord who has been my Guide all the way.

Simply Following

Acknowledgements

"You must write your story," many friends and supporters have often said to me. I suppose these comments were the seed that produced this book. I regret that the names of many dear friends, co-workers, and family members do not appear in this concise summary of my life. I think especially of some who have enriched my retirement years, but I cannot possibly mention them all in this book.

I do want to express heart-felt gratitude to those who have directly helped produce this book. Wesley Skinner graciously provided funding which made this printing possible. Publisher Dan Runyon went far beyond the call of duty by encouraging me to write and giving valuable counsel at every step in bringing the book to completion. Muriel Teusink put the text on computer. Tim Kratzer provided the cover photo. Sally Trevan, Renee Runyon, Harold and Ella Munn, Paula Innes and Leota Meyers helped in the final stages of proof-reading and editing.

Most of all, my gratitude and praise belong to Christ whom I have been simply following all the way.